PYTHON PROGRAMMING

2 IN 1 ULTIMATE

VALUE PYTHON GUIDE

Also by Ronald Olsen

∿∿∿∿∿∿∿∿∿∿∿∿∿∿∿∿∿∿∿∿∿∿

Raspberry PI: The Only Essential Quick & Easy Book You Need To Start Your Own Raspberry Projects Immediately

See more books: **https://www.auvapress.com/books**

Leave a review on Amazon:

https://www.auvapress.com/amazon-review/python-programming-2in1

2 IN 1 ULTIMATE VALUE PYTHON GUIDE

PYTHON
PROGRAMMING

- LEARN PYTHON SERIES -

RONALD OLSEN

AUVA PRESS

FIRST EDITION

ISBN-13: 978-1-9759-3163-6
ISBN-10: 1-9759-3163-7

Copy Editor: Betty Oakes, Kelly Pam
Cover Designer: Terrence Reese
Development Editor: Peter Nathan
Technical Reviewer: Tony Richards

For my friends and family,
who make my world more meaningful

CONTENTS

PART I: LEARN PYTHON IN A DAY AND

MASTER IT WELL

The Only Essential Book You Need To Start
Programming In Python Now!

Abstract

The computing world has undergone a remarkable revolution in recent times. During this time, programming languages have changed, too. It's no secret that robust, more efficient, and easy-to-learn object-oriented programming languages such as C++, JavaScript, Java, Golang, Perl etc. have emerged as an alternative to the core and structural languages such as C and FORTRAN.

In spite of being a general-purpose programming language (Python can be applied in web development, mobile, and desktop apps), Python language is simple to learn. It's also a very flexible programming language that has been used to develop some of the coolest e-commerce and web applications. Being an object oriented language, you'll also be on your way to learning other languages such as Java, Golang, and Perl if you finish reading this book.

This book is meant to help you, the novice programmers, gain an understanding of Python programming. Whether you're new to Python or even new to programming, you'll find this book helpful in fast-tracking your understanding of Python language. The book has been written to enable novice programmers to get started as soon as possible. Written by an experienced computer scientist, **Learn Python in A Day and Master It Well** is a comprehensive guide for beginners. This book will teach you all the principles and concepts of Python programming through in a simple and succinct language.

You'll acquire Python programming skills that are necessary for the practical development of applications in real-world scenarios. Throughout the chapters, you'll find Python code samples that illustrate the concepts of Python programming. At the end of each chapter, you'll find exercises that test and challenge your understanding of Python. The solutions to these exercises have been provided at the end of the chapter, fast-tracking your knowledge and understanding of Python language.

By the time you finish reading this book, you'll be a professional Python programmer with in-depth knowledge and experience of creating your own Python software. It is my hope that you'll enjoy the book. Good luck!

The odds are, if you've bought this book, then you're a newbie to Python. Or, you could be new to programming altogether. In either case, you've made the right decision by choosing Python programming language.

In the last couple of decades, the programming environment has witnessed a momentous growth in the number of languages. We've seen how core programming languages such as C, FORTRAN, and COBOL evolved in 1960's and 1970's to address programmers' challenges. But in recent times, we've also seen how object-oriented programming languages such as C++, JavaScript, Java, and even Golang have emerged as an alternative to core programming languages. In all these developments, the Python language has stood out distinctively from the rest.

Why Python?

Well, Python language is a fully-functional programming language. This means that the language can perform almost anything that any programming language can do in a cost effective and efficient manner. Python language is capable of threading and GPU, graphical processing, just like any other programming language such as Java, C++, and Golang. In fact, most of the processing is handled in modules that are already pre-written that just need importation for use.

Therefore, if you're a newbie to Python, or even new to programming, you'll find these modules helpful in developing programs within the shortest time possible. If you're good in C++, you'll find programming in Python to be simple. This is because the Python code can be wrapped around C++ codes for seamless interaction. By using C++ codes, you'll be in a position to use various tools of C++ without having to understand the language.

But that's not all.

Python language is beginner-friendly, yet very powerful. In fact, the syntax, rules defining the structure of statements, is extremely simple to understand and follow. You don't need any experience in programming to begin coding in Python! Because of its powerful nature, Python has been used to develop some of the most popular applications such as Google, Pinterest, Mozilla, SurveyMonkey, SlideShare, YouTube, and Reddit.

It's also used to develop games, perform data analysis, control the robot and hardware, and create GUIs. This means that there are several career options that demand Python language. Thus, learning Python can be the greatest asset to land that dream job! You may also boost your career with new Python programming skills.

This book will provide you with all the vital programming concepts and skills that are necessary for you learn Python. It will walk you through the comprehensive step-by-step instructions that are necessary for you to create your own software. Without further ado, let's jump in and learn Python!

Chapter 1

Understanding Python

Welcome to the world of programming in Python language. This chapter provides you with the ins and outs of Python language. By the end of the chapter, you'll have understood the bigger picture of Python language.

Are you ready?

Good.

Let's begin with the most important question—what is Python?

What is Python?

Well, Python language is a high-level, interpreted, and object-oriented programming language with dynamic semantics. Being a high-level programming language, you can easily construct statements using a syntax that's easy to learn. In fact, the core philosophy of Python is to allow programmers to write codes that are not only readable but also minimize maintenance routines.

Besides, its high-level inbuilt data structures make it a perfect candidate for Rapid Application Development. The language supports the use of modules and packages that encourage modularity and code reuse (object oriented paradigms), which can accelerate the development of software. The Python interpreter and all the standard libraries are available in binary format for all the major platforms such as Windows, Linux, and Mac OS. These source codes are open source and, therefore, are freely distributed.

I fell in love with Python because of the increased productivity it provides. Python is an interpreted language, therefore, there's is no compilation step process required. This means that the edit-test-debug process will be incredibly fast compared to other programming languages such as Java and C++. In fact, a bug or any bad input in the Python code can never cause the whole software to fail. Instead, the interpreter will raise an exception or print a stack trace that provides clues on the source of the bug in the code.

Next up, let's examine the versions of Python language.

Versions of Python language

The Python language was invented in the late 1980's by Guido van Rossum in the Netherlands as a successor to ABC programming language. Since its first release, there have been major improvements starting with the version 1.0, 1.5, and 1.6. In October 2000, Python version 2 was released as a garbage collection management system that is capable of collecting the reference cycles.

The initial version of Python 2 (Python 2.1) was almost similar to Python 1.5. All the codes, documentation, and specifications that were added, starting with Python 2.1, is owned by Python Software Foundation (PSF)—an umbrella organization formed in 2001 to regulate future releases of Python versions. The PSF focused on regulating the language specification and the nested scopes.

In November 2014, PSF announced that Python 2.7, the latest and final version of Python 2, would be supported until 2020.

The current version of Python is Python 3. Users are advised to install the latest version of Python. However, if you're using Python 2.7, then you have until 2020. Beyond 2020, Python 2.7 will be no longer supported. At the time of writing this book, the latest version of Python was 3.6. Python 3.6 was released in December 2016.

So, which version should you use?

Now, the most appropriate version of Python to use depends on what you want to get done by the language. If you can do exactly want you to get done with Python 2.7, then it's great! However, there will be few demerits ranging from library support and the operating system platform support. As long as Python 3 is installed on your computer, then you shouldn't worry because most of the libraries will be supported. For instance, in the majority of Linux distributions, Python 3.x will be already installed.

Professionally speaking, I advise you to go for the latest version of Python, which is Python 3.6. This is because Python 3.6 removes many problems that can hinder your programming capabilities. Major packages that have been ported to the latest version of Python 3 are:

- The NumPy and SciPy, which are used for number processing and scientific computing
- The Django, the Flask, the CherryPy and Pyramid, which are used for websites
- The PIL, which is an image processing module
- The cx_Freeze, which is used for packaging the applications with their dependencies
- The py2exe, which is used for packaging Python application for Windows users

- The OpenCV 3, which is used in machine learning
- The lxml, which is a powerful and Pythonic XML processing library

For whom is this book written?

It's a fact that Python programming language is currently one of the most popular programming languages for developing modern data-driven websites, doing data analysis, and software development. By the end of the year 2015, Python language was already topping the list of programming languages that serious programmers were interested in learning.

In fact, a study conducted by Hired.com revealed that Python language recorded a whopping 40.4% popularity, topping Java programming language for the first time in two decades. This was followed by Java, JavaScript Front-end, HTML/CSS, and Ruby in that order. Whether you're new to Python or you're new to programming, you've made the right decision.

This book is intended for programmers who would like to master Python programming language. If you're interested in the following job profiles, then this book is for you:

- Software Engineer
- Research Analyst
- Data Analyst
- Data Scientist

- Software Developer

What you can expect to learn

The introductory chapter of this book explores the big picture view of Python programming language. In this chapter, you'll learn all the basics of Python language including the two renowned versions of Python, Python 2 and Python 3, and applications of Python language in business, finance, and web and mobile applications.

Chapter 2 will teach you all the basics of Python language, including all the steps that are required to get you started, including, but not limited to, how to install Python language on any platform, the text editors, and the IDLE environment. Once you're done with this chapter, you'll be in a position to start programming in Python.

In chapter 3, you'll learn the variables and data types in Python language. Chapter 4 will walk you through all the Python operators, including the Basics Operators, Logical Operators, Arithmetic Operators, and Comparison Operators. Chapter 5 will introduce you to list data structure, where you'll learn how to change, add, and remove elements in a list. You'll also learn how to organize and sort lists.

In chapter 6, we explore the decision structures in Python language. These include the If else statement, While loops, and

Switch statements. Chapter 7 will teach you all the Python functions and modules. Chapter 8 will introduce the concept of classes in Python programming language while chapter 9 will teach you all the common error and exception techniques in Python. Finally, you'll learn the basics of testing your Python application in chapter 10.

Why Python language?

You've heard that familiar advice that university or college education will equip you with the right tools required to succeed to land that dream job. However, when you enroll for any course in computers, whether computer science, software engineer, or IT, you'll discover that the curriculum for most of these courses is theoretical. This means that when you graduate, you'll still be ill-equipped to enter the job market.

In the programming world, you can begin to study some of the top-notch programming languages on your own. But truth be told, there are very few programming languages that are easy to learn. And Python is one of them! With Python language, it's never too late.

You can't be too old or too young to begin learning the language. Here are compelling justifications for why Python programming language should your first sortie into programming world:

#1: Simple to learn

Let's face it, learning any programming language isn't a walk in the park. However, Python language was designed with newbies in mind. In fact, the syntax is as simple to understand and follow as kindergarten math. You don't need any experience in programming to begin coding in Python. The use of white spaces and other common expressions have eliminated the need for mind-numbing variable declarations and the distasteful curly brackets.

The language has been designed around the philosophy of "less code" that completes basic tasks. This makes Python language to be one of the most economical languages you can ever learn on the planet. As a matter of fact, the Python language is almost three to five times shorter than Java language and five to ten times shorter than C++.

#2: It can be your stepping stone to learning other languages

Mastering the Python language can be your stepping stone into the world of programming. Being object oriented, just like Java, JavaScript, C++, or Perl, Python language can help you learn other programming languages. If you're planning to become a top-rated software developer, which I bet you are, then you should invest in Python language. It can easily help you to invest in other programming environments.

#3: It has vast capabilities for web development

It is no secret that web development is still a booming economic venture for most programmers. With Python's vast web development capabilities, you can become an effective web developer. For instance, Django, the renowned open source web development framework that's written in Python, is the bedrock of some of the most popular sites such as Pinterest, the Guardian, the New York Times, and Instagram.

Being open source means that all the information that you need to capitalize on Django will be found online at www.DjangoProject.com. Additionally, web development with the Django framework will always document because it has a vast support community. In fact, one of the reasons you should consider learning Python is its ability to allow you to program within the shortest time.

#4: It is flexible

Being a dynamically typed language, Python is very flexible. There are no difficult standard rules on how to build the features, therefore, you'll be more flexible when solving problems related to desktop and web apps. Furthermore, the Python language is really forgiving when it comes to debugging. A bug or any bad input in the Python code can never cause the whole software to fail.

Instead, the interpreter will raise an exception or print a stack trace that provides clues on the source of the bug in the code. In fact, you'll still be in a position to compile and run the Python code until the problematic part is encountered.

#5: It is general-purpose language

Python is a general-purpose programming language, which implies it can be used to code just about anything ranging from desktop to web applications, data mining, and scientific computing. This has been made by the right libraries and tools that are offered in package form in the language. However, it's important to note that Python language is great for the development of backend systems, performing data analysis, artificial intelligence, and scientific computing.

Applications of Python programming language

Python programming language can be applied in the following areas:

#1: Business and e-commerce

In recent times, the numbers of online storefronts have grown exponentially, causing the online marketplaces to become overcrowded. Some of these storefronts have exposed businesses to serious challenges ranging from response times, security, and scalability. The Django, a Python language framework for the development of intensive data-driven websites, has come in handy in helping web developers to build fast, secure, and scalable e-commerce websites.

Among the popular websites that have been created using the Django framework are:

- Survey Monkey
- Reddit
- Pinterest
- Reddit Gifts
- Playfire

#2: Financial technology

Python language is used in Blockchain technology for the development of smart contracts, computer protocols that facilitate, enforce, and verify negotiations and performance of contracts. The smart contracts describe codes that are capable of executing and enforcing negotiations and agreements.

#3: Mobile Applications

Mobile app development has become a huge industry with a lot of promising capabilities to software developers around the world. Even though Python language isn't very developed when it comes to the development of native applications, its web applications features are necessary for the development of web applications, for both Android and iOS smartphones, that aren't hybrid or native.

Chapter 2

Python Basics

Welcome to Python basics. This chapter provides you with a big picture view of Python basics, including details of how you can install it, Python text editors, Python IDLE, and an overview of Python application. So, let's dive in.

The installation process

The process of downloading and installing the Python language interpreter is pretty simple. If you're using the latest Linux distribution, whether Ubuntu, Fedora, or Linux Mint, then you'll find the latest version of Python installed. However, for other operating system platforms, you have to download and install Python yourself.

How to install Python on Linux distributions

Python is an open source programming language, which means it's freely available. For most Linux distributions, you'll find the Python language already installed. To check whether Python has been installed on any Linux distribution, simply open the Terminal as root and type: python at the command prompt. Press the enter key.

If you see something starting, then it's Python, which means it has already been installed. However, if you don't see anything, then it means you haven't installed Python. It's time to install. Let's dive in and find out how you can install Python.

Below are steps necessary for installing Python on Linux OS systems:

- Launch the Terminal (Ensure you're connected to the Internet)
- Type "su" at the command prompt and press the enter key
- Type your root password and hit the enter key
- If you're using Debian-based Linux distribution such as Ubuntu, then type: "apt-get install python" at the command prompt and press the enter key
- If you're using the Red Hat/RHEL/CentOS Linux distributions such as Fedora, then type: "yum install python" at the command prompt and hit the enter key.
- Wait for the installation process to complete.
- If you're using Debian-based Linux distribution such as Ubuntu, then type: "apt-get update" at the command

prompt and press the enter key for the Python to get updated to the latest version.
- If you're using the Red Hat/RHEL/CentOS Linux distributions such as Fedora, then type: "yum update" at the command prompt and hit the enter key. This ensures that your Python software has been updated to the latest version.

And there you have it! You have just installed Python interpreter on your computer. It's simple, isn't it?

How to install Python on Windows OS

Before you download and install Python, decide on the version of Python language you would want to install. As a rule of thumb, always go for the latest version. In this case, the latest version is Python 3.6. Below are steps that can help you install Python on Windows OS:

- Go to www.python.org and download the latest version of Python. Select the appropriate version depending on the nature of your operating system (32 bit, or 64 bit).
- Open the Python file you've just downloaded
- Click on the "Accept the default settings" from the on-screen instructions and wait for the installation process to complete.

What about Mac OS?

How to install Python on Mac OS

The latest versions of Mac OS X and Sierra have Python 2.7 already ported in them. Therefore, you don't have to install or configure anything if you want to begin using Python. However, if you wish to install the latest version of Python, you need to use the Homebrew.

Here are steps that can help install Python on Mac OS:

> - Open your Terminal or any of your favorite OSX terminal emulator
> - Type the following command at the command prompt: "/user/bin/ruby-e"$(curl-fsSL https://raw.githubusercontent.com/Homebrew/install/master/install)".
> - Wait for the app to be installed.
> - Once the installation process has completed, insert the Homebrew directory at the top of the PATH environment variable. You can perform this operation by adding the following line at the bottom of the "~/.profile" file: "export PATH=/usr/local/bin: /usr/local/sbin: $PATH"
> - Now proceed to install Python language interpreter by typing the following command at the command prompt: "brew install python."
> - Wait for the installation process to complete.

Now that you've installed Python, what next?

Well, it's now time to begin programming. But not so fast! You should decide on what text editor you'll use. Let's explore the text editors in Python programming.

Text Editors

Just as the name suggests, a text editor is simply a program that you'll use to type and execute your Python language statements. In other words, the text editor will help you to write the Python code. It also has the features that will help you with common tasks such as auto-indentation and automatic code formatting when writing the code. But if you don't want to use any text editor, you can use the Python programming shell. The Python Shell allows programmers to run the Python language commands line by line.

The following are some of the text editors that you can use with Python:

- **Emacs**. Emacs is a popular text editor that runs on Windows, Mac OS X, Linux, and even Android distributions.
- **Geany**. Geany is a cross-platform text editor that provides the most basic features of any IDE. It has Python syntax highlighting features such as auto-indentation, although it doesn't provide auto-indentation after return and the break statements.
- **Komodo Edit**. Komodo Edit provides the following features: Auto-indentation, project and code navigation, code folding, Auto-completion, and Snippets.

- **Notepad++.** Notepad++ is at basic text editor with few features that you can rely upon when programming in Python. It has the acceptable syntax highlighting, but that is all it provides.

- **SciTE**. SciTE is a light and fast and easy to learn text editor, just like the Geany.

- **Sublime Text**. This has an outstanding selection of powerful features that includes multiple cursors a flexible "goto anything" and a command palette that allows easy access to keyboard features.

Inasmuch as the text editors will help you to write the Python codes, you'll still have to run them manually from Python shell. In fact, when you use the text editor, you have to save the file using the ".py" extension and run the file from the Python shell. If you want to write complex Python scripts and run them at once, you'll need the IDLE.

Let's explore the Python's IDLE

Python IDLE

IDLE (Integrated Development and Learning Environment) is an integrated development environment for the Python interpreter. It has been ported to the latest version of Python interpreter. In Linux distributions, it's packaged as an optional part of the Python package. IDLE is intended to provide a simple IDE for accelerated development of Python programs. Among the features you'll get when you install IDLE are:

- Syntax highlighting
- Auto-completion
- Smart indentation
- Integrated debugger with the stepping, persistent breakpoints, and call stack visibility features.

IDLE has two basic types of window: the Shell window and the Editor window. The shell window provides you with capabilities of typing and running the Python codes on the Python shell while the Editor window allows you to capitalize on the IDLE features such as syntax highlighting, auto completion, and smart indentation.

I know you're wondering, "How can I install the Python IDLE?"

Good question.

If you're using Debian-based Linux distribution systems such as Ubuntu, open the Terminal and type the following command at the command prompt: "sudo apt-get install idle3" and hit the enter key. You'll be prompted to provide the root password. Type in your root password, press the enter key, and wait for the installation process to complete.

Similarly, if you're using Red Hat/RHEL/CentOS Linux distributions such as Fedora, open the Terminal and type the following command at the command prompt: "sudo yum install idle3" and hit the enter key. You'll be prompted to provide the root password. Type in your root password, press the enter key, and wait for the installation process to complete.

If you're using Windows OS, go to www.python.org and download the latest version of Python IDLE. Select the appropriate version depending on the nature of your operating system. Once you've downloaded the app, open the file and follow the onscreen instructions to install Python IDLE.

If you are a Mac user, go to www.python.org and download the latest version of Python IDLE. Select the appropriate version depending on the nature of your Mac system. Once you've downloaded the app, open the file and follow the onscreen instructions to install Python IDLE.

So far, so good. We've now explored the basic features of Python language. It's now time to get started. Keep reading.

Getting started with Python

To get started, you have to figure out how to launch the Python app.

So, how can you launch Python?

It's simple. If you're a Windows user, go to Start>Programs and click on Python. If you're a Mac user, launch the Terminal and type: "python" at the command prompt. Similarly, if you are a Linux user, simply open the Terminal and type: "python" at the command prompt.

Now that you've launched the Python, it's now time to begin coding.

Let's now create our first program in Python. Follow these steps to write your first Python program:

- Open the Python Shell.
- Write the Python language statements (instructions) in the shell.
- Run the program

That's it! Isn't it simple?

Now, here's a quick way to see the programming process in action...Proceed and copy/paste the following code into your Python Shell.

```
Print ("Hello World! This is my first program")
```

Run the program. What do you see as the output?

Well, the phrase "Hello World! This is my first program" appears.

Congratulations! You've just written your first Python code. At this time, don't worry so much about the meaning of statements. I'll explain the technical details in the following sections.

An Overview of Python Application

Now that you have executed your first Python program, what else do you need to know? Well, it's now time to understand the vital components of any Python code, including its structure.

Structure of Python programs

Python programs have the following structure:

```
import sys

def main ():

main ()

{

Program statements

}
```

As you can see from the above program structure, Python code should always start with the keyword "*import*". Now, *what are we importing?*

Remember, Python language is object-oriented. Therefore, it has components of all the object-oriented programming languages. One such property is inheritance. The ability to inherit features of codes in Python allows programmers to reuse pieces of codes that had been written elsewhere. Technically speaking, the import statement tells the Python interpreter to declare classes that have already been used in other Python packages without referring to their full package names.

For instance, the statement: "import sys" informs the interpreter to include all the system libraries such as print whenever the Python program is starting.

What does the statement "def main ( ):" mean?

Whenever any Python program is loaded and run, the computer's memory, the Random Access Memory, contains the objects with function definitions. The function definitions provide the programmers with the capabilities of instructing the control unit to place the function object into the appropriate section of the computer's memory. In other words, it's like instructing the control unit to check the main memory and initialize the program that needs to be executed.

The function objects in the memory can be specified using names. That's where the statement "def main ( ):" comes in. It simply tells the control unit to start executing the Python code statements that are placed immediately after the statement "def main ( ):"

For example, the Python code below creates a function object and assigns it the name "main":

```
def main ():

  if len (sys.argv) == 10:

   name = sys.argv [2]

  else:

   name = "My World"

  print ("Hello"), name
```

In the above code, the Python interpreter will run all the function statements in the Python file by placing the set of functions objects in the memory and linking each of them with the namespace. This will happen when the program is initialized with the import statement.

But more fundamentally, "What are the different elements of Python code?"

Well, all Python programs have the following components:

- *Documenting the program*. Any statement in the program (except the first) that starts with "#" is treated as a command line or comment line and will be ignored during execution. This will allow you to comment on sections of the code for proper documentation.

- *Keywords*. The keywords are instructions that the interpreter recognizes and understands. For instance, the word "print" in the earlier program is a keyword. In Python, there are two main types of keywords: the functions and the control keywords. Functions are simply verbs such as print that tell the interpreter what to do while the control keywords control the flow of execution. Examples of keywords are: and, Del, from, not, while, as, elif, global, or, with, assert, else, if, pass, break, except, import, print, class, return, def, for, etc. It is a must for you to respect the keywords, and not use them as normal names in your Python program.

- *Modules*. Python program is shipped with a large list of modules that increases its functionality. The modules will help you to organize your code in a manner that's easy to debug and control the code.

- *Program statements*. The program statements are sentences or instructions that tell the control unit to perform a given operation. Unlike most programming languages, the Python statements don't need a semicolon at the end.

- **White space**. The white spaces are a collective name that given to tabs, the spaces, and new lines/carriage returns. The Python language is strict on where the white space should be placed in the code.
- Escape sequences. The escape sequences are special characters used for output. For instance, the sequence "\n" in the program tells Python to output on a new line.

There you have it. You're on the right track to becoming an expert in Python programming. In the next chapter, we explore more about Python programming by explaining variables and types.

Chapter 3

Variables and Data Types

Are you ready to explore on variables and data types in Python? Fantastic. There's so much that goes on in the main memory of the computer whenever you run a program. Understanding the concept of variables and data types will help you to write efficient programs. So, let's jump in.

To understand what a variable is, we need to define the term program.

A program, like the one you wrote in the previous chapter, is simply a sequence of instructions (statements) that directs your computer to perform a particular task. For instance, the previous program printed the phrase "Hello World! This is my first program" on the screen when it was executed. But before you could see the output on the screen, some data had to be kept in computer's memory.

The use of data applies to all programming languages, Python included, therefore, understanding the mechanisms of data management in the computer's memory is the first step towards developing robust, efficient, and powerful applications.

But first, what exactly is a variable?

A variable can be conceived as a temporary storage location in the computer's main memory and, specifically, the Random Access Memory. This temporary storage location is what will hold the data that you would like to use in the program. In other words, the variable location of memory that holds data whenever your program is executing. So, whenever you define a variable, you'll actually be reserving a temporary storage location in the computer's memory.

Now, all the variables you define must have names and an equivalent data type, a sort of classification of the variable that specifies the type of value the variable should hold. The data types help to specify what sort of mathematical, relational, or even logical operations you can apply to the variable without causing an error. Ideally, when you assign variables to data types, you can begin to store numbers, characters, and even constants in the computer's main memory. Because Python language is an oriented programming language, it is not "statically typed". This means the interpreter regards every variable as an object. Therefore, you have to declare the variables before using them in your program. So, how can you declare variables in Python?

Good question.

Python variables are usually declared by names or identifiers. Just like any other programming languages you have so far learned, the conventions for naming the variables must strictly be adhered to. Below are some naming conventions you should follow when declaring variables:

- All variable names should always begin with a letter (A to Z and a to z) or an underscore. For instance, "age" is a valid variable name whereas "-age" isn't a valid variable name.
- Any variable name you declare cannot start with a number. For instance, 9age is not a valid variable name.
- Special symbols shouldn't be used when declaring variable names. For instance, @name isn't allowed as a variable name.
- The maximum number of characters to use for your variable name shouldn't exceed 255.

I know you're now asking, "How can I assign specific values to variables in Python?"

How to assign values to Variables in Python

To reserve a temporary memory location in the name of a variable, you don't have to use the explicit declaration like other programming languages. If you've had experience in other programming languages such as Pascal or C, I am sure you know that declaring a variable explicitly before assigning any value is a must.

In Python, the declaration of variables usually occurs automatically the moment you assign a value to it. We use the equal sign "=" to assign values to variables. For instance, the statement

```
age=10
```

Aautomatically reserves a temporary storage location in memory space called "age" and assigns 10 to it.

It is also possible to assign a single value to several variables simultaneously. For instance, the statement below reserves temporary memory spaces for 2 variables, namely, age and count and assigns them value 30:

```
age, count=30
```

Data types that are supported in Python

Python language has different categories of data types that are used to define the storage methods and mathematical operations. Below are examples data types in Python language:

- Numbers
- String
- List
- Tuple
- Dictionary

Let's explore these data types in detail.

#1: Numbers

The Number data types stores numeric values. The number objects will automatically be initialized whenever you assign a specific value to the variable. For instance, the code illustrated below creates 2 variable objects (age and count) and assigns them the values 10 and 30 respectively:

```
age = 10

count= 30
```

If you want to delete reference to the Number object, you'll use the word "del" followed by the variable name you wish to delete. Consider the code below that deletes two variables: age and count that have already been declared and used.

```
del age, count
```

Python language supports four different categories of number types. These are:

- Int. When used in a declaration, it refers to signed integers. These include those whole numbers that range from 8 bits to 32 bits.
- Long. These are long integers. They can be represented either in octal and hexadecimal numbering notation.
- Float. These are floating real point values. They may range from 8 bits to 64 bits long.
- Complex. These are complex numbers.

Below is an example Python code that uses number data types:

```
mynum = 10

print ("The Number you have just typed is an Integer: %d" %
mynum)
```

#2: Strings

Strings are stored as consecutive sets of characters in the computer's memory locations. Python language allows you to use either pair of single or double quotes when defining the strings. Other subsets of string variable types can be specified using the slice operator ([ ] and the [:]) with the indexes that range from 0 at the beginning of the string.

The plus (+) operator performs string concatenation (joining of two or more strings) while the asterisk (*) operator performs string repetition. Below is an example of a Python code that uses strings:

```
mystring = "Welcome to Python programming."

print mystring     # This statement prints the complete string:
"Welcome to Python programming."

print mystring [0]    # this statement prints out the first
character of the string:"W"

print mystring [2:5]   # this statement prints characters
beginning from the third to the fifth: "lco"

print mystring [3:] # Prints string starting from the fourth
character: "Welcome to Python programming."

print mystring * 2    # this statement prints the string two times:
"Welcome to Python programming." "Welcome to Python
programming."

print mystring + "in Python" #this statement prints the
concatenated string: "Welcome to Python programming in
Python"
```

#3: Lists

If you're familiar with arrays in C programming language, then lists are no different. However, unlike arrays in C, Python lists can contain items that do not necessarily belong to the same data type. The list items are separated by commas and enclosed in square brackets ([]). Lists are declared by providing their names and initializing them with specific data values. Here is an example:

```
myList = ["Stars", "Jupiter", "Earth", "Moon", "Mars", "Pluto", "Saturn"]
```

For you to access the individual elements in a list, you'll use the same notation that's provided in arrays. For instance:

```
myList [0] # Is the first item in the list, which is Stars.

myList [2] # Is the third item in the list, which is Earth.

myList [5] # Is the sixth item in the list, which is Pluto.
```

Changing, Adding, and Removing elements in a list

The methods "insert", "append", and "extend" can be used to modify the contents of the list. The insert method requires that the index and the value to be added to the list are known in advance. For example, the Python code below shows how the insert method can be used to add an element in a list at index 2:

```
myList. insert (2, "Mercury")
```

The append method picks one or more list elements as an input and adds them to the existing list. Here's an example:

myList. Append (["Sun", "Moon"])

The other method used for adding elements to an existing list is the extend method. Just like the append method, this method requires one or more values as an input. However, unlike the append method, all the data elements are added as individual elements. Here's an example:

myList.extend (["Stars", "Meteors"])

The list can also be searched for values using an index method. The index method should specify the value to be searched where the output is the index at the location where the value has been kept. Here is an example of a code that searches for the element "Saturn" in myList:

myList.index ("Earth")

The delete method is used to remove list items from a Python list. Here is an example of Python code that removes an item "Saturn" from myList:

myList. Remove ("Saturn")

Organizing and Sorting of List items

Sorting of list items is handled by the sort () method. The method sort () sorts list items using the compare function. Below is the syntax of the sort () method:

```
list.sort([func])
```

The above method doesn't return any value but only reverses the given list items. Below is an example of how you can sort the list.

```
MyList = [50, 2, 340, 58, 63,603]

MyList. Sort ()

Print ("The sorted list is:", MyList)
```

When you run the above program, it will produce the following output:

The sorted list is: 2,50,58,63,340,603

Note the above function sorts the list items in ascending order. How about sorting the list items in descending order?

We'll use the same sort () method, but include the reverse function. Here's is the syntax:

Sort (reverse =True)

Take a look at the example code below:

```
MyList = [50, 2, 340, 58, 63,603];

MyList. Sort (reverse=True)

Print ("The sorted list is:", MyList)
```

Now, here is the output of the above code:

The sorted list is: 603, 340, 63, 58, 50, 2

Multi-dimensional lists in Python

The lists we've described so far are one dimensional. Multi-dimensional lists are simply lists that are contained within other lists. Efficient programmers can use Dictionaries (we'll explain dictionaries later) to define lists. But if you're familiar with multi-dimensional arrays in programming languages such as C, you should not have any problem.

Consider the example below:

MyList = [[5, 2], [6, 2], [3, 1], [12, 6]]

Now, with nested lists, we can easily create a lookup table or row lengths that produce different rows with each row having a different number of list elements. How do you go about it?

Well, you'll create an empty list and add other empty lists to it using the append () method. This way, you'll have built a 2 by 2 multidimensional list. Here's how you can go about it:

```
MyList = []# Define an empty list.

MyList. Append([])# Append the empty lists in the first two indexes.

MyList. Append([])
```

```
MyList[0].append(1) # Now begin to add elements to the empty
lists.

MyList[0].append(2)

MyList [1].append(3)

MyList [1].append(4)

print(MyList [0][0]) # Here's how you'll display the top-left
element.

print(MyList) # Here's how you'll display the entire list.
```

#4: Tuples

Python tuples are a number of values separated by commas.
But unlike the lists, where the elements and sizes of the lists
can be changed, the tuples must be enclosed within the
parentheses and they can't be updated. For instance, the
Python code below creates a tuple known as months:

```
months =
("Jan","Feb","Mar","Apr","May","June","July","Aug","Sept","Oct","N
ov","Dec")
```

Below is an example of Python code demonstrating the use of
tuples:

```
print months # Prints the complete tuple
```

```
print months[0]      # Prints first element of the tuple

print months[1:3]     # Prints elements starting from the second
to the third

print months [2:]      # Prints elements that starting from the
third element

print months * 2   # Prints tuple two times

print months + months # Prints the concatenated tuple
```

#5: Dictionaries

A Dictionary is a data structure that operates in a similar manner to the hash tables. The hash tables are simply an array of information with key-valued pairs. The Python dictionaries are associative arrays, or hashes, that have key-valued pairs where the dictionary key can take any Python data type. However, numbers or strings are the most common methods of defining the dictionary keys. However, the dictionary values can take any arbitrary Python object.

Python Dictionaries are enclosed by the curly brackets ({ }), and the values are assigned and accessed using the square brackets ([]). Here's an example code:

```
mydictionary = {}

mydictionary["One"] = "This is 1."
```

```
mydictionary[2]    = "This is 2"

smalldictionary = {"name": "Ronald Olsen", "code":722848386,
"dept": "IT"}
```

Here's an example an illustration of Python Dictionaries:

```
print mydictionary["one"]    # Prints the value for "one" key

print mydictionary[2]        # Prints the value for 2 key

print smalldictionary        # Prints the complete dictionary

print smalldictionary.keys()  # Prints all the keys
```

Now, let's explore type casting, which is somehow related to variables and data types.

Types and casting in Python

Typecasting allows Python programmers to convert an entity from one data type to another. For instance, you may want to convert a string data type such as "2000" to a number type. But why do you need type casting in Python?"

You may want to take advantage of certain properties of a particular object data type. For instance, you may declare a string variable data type that has the operations of "+ and *) as we have learned earlier in our previous section on strings. But you may want to apply number operations such as "/, - and |."

For you achieve numerical operations on such a data type, you have to convert it, or typecast such a variable, to a number.

To cast between the different data types, you must specify the data type name as the function. There are several built-in functions that can help you to convert from one data type to another. Examples of these functions are:

- int(x [base]). It converts the value x to an integer where the base defined is a string or not.
- long(x [base]). It converts the value x to the long integer where the base specified is x a string or not.
- float(x). It converts the value x to floating point number.
- complex (real [imag]). It produces a complex number.
- str(x). It converts the object x to string data type.
- eval(str). It evaluates the string and returns the object.
- tuple(x). It converts the value x to a tuple.
- list(x). It converts the value x to a list.
- set(x). It converts the value x to a set.
- dict(x). It converts the value x to a dictionary where x must be a sequence of the (key, value) tuples.
- chr(x). It converts the integer to a character.
- unichr(x). It converts an integer to the Unicode character.
- ord(x). It converts the single character to its integer value.

- hex(x). It converts an integer to a hexadecimal string.
- oct(x). It converts an integer to an octal string.

Have a look at the example of the code below. What do you think will be the output?

```
a = "3000"

b = "2000"

print (x + y)

print int(x) + int(y)
```

The output of the above code will be:

```
3000-2000

4000
```

Can you explain why the output is like that? Well, the first statement (print x+y) will display a concatenation of two strings: 3000 and 2000. In the second statement, the x variable has been converted to integer data type. Similarly, the second variable has also been converted to integer data type. Thus, the statement print (x+y) prints the sum of x and y, which is 4000.

Are you ready for exercises?

Let's see.

Chapter 3 - Fun Exercises

Exercise 1

Write a Python program that accepts the base and height of the triangle as inputs and compute the area.

Exercise 2

Write a Python program which gets from the keyboard which is made the first 2 and the last 2 characters. If the length of the string is less than 2, then the program should return a value. Otherwise, it should return an empty string.

For instance, if you type "'w3resource", the program should display "w3ce" and if you type w3, the program should display "w3"

Exercise 3

Write a Python program that displays a specified list after removing the 0th, 2nd, 4th and 5th elements.

For instance if the sample list has the following elements: ["John", "Peter","Sam", "Tim", "Janet", "Dan"] the expected output will be: ["Peter", "Tim"]

Exercise 4

Write a Python program that concatenates following dictionaries into a new one dictionary:

dictionary1= {1:20, 4:40}

dictionary2= {6:60, 8:80}

dictionary3= {10:100, 12:120}

The expected result: {2: 20, 4: 40, 6: 60, 8: 80, 10: 100, 12: 120}

Exercise 5

Write Python programs that sum all the items in the list.

Exercise 6

What is the output of the following code?

```
from datetime import date

first_date = date(2014, 7, 2)

last_date = date(2014, 7, 11)

n = last_date - first_date

print(n.days)
```

Solution for Exercise 1

A triangle is any polygon that has 3 edges and three vertices. The code below illustrates how you can compute the area of the triangle:

```
base = int(input("Input the value of the base :"))   #Enter the base of the triangle

height = int(input("Input the value of the height :"))  #Enter the height of the triangle

area = base*height/2  # Formula for computing the area

print(" The area of the triangle is =", area)  #Display the area of the triangle
```

Solution for Exercise 2

```
import sys

def main ():

main ()

{def strings_onboth_ends(str):

  if len(str) < 2:

    return ""

 return str[0:2] + str[-2:]

print(strings_onboth_ends ("w3resource"))

print(strings_onboth_ends ("w3"))

print(strings_onboth_ends ("w"))

}
```

Solution for Exercise 3

```
import sys

def main ():

main ()

{

Peoples_names = ["John", "Peter","Sam", "Tim", "Janet", "Dan"]

Peoples_names = [x for (i, x) in enumerate (Peoples_names) if i
not in (0, 4, 5)]

print (Peoples_names)

}
```

Solution for Exercise 4

```
import sys

def main ():

main ()

{

dictionary1= {1:20, 4:40}

dictionary2= {6:60, 8:80}

dictionary3= {10:100, 12:120}

dicionary4 = {}

for d in (dictionary1, dictionary2, dictionary3):
dictionary4.update(d)

print(dictionary4)

}
```

Solution for Exercise 5

```
def sum_oflist(items):

    sum_ofnumbers = 0

    for n in items:

        sum_ofnumbers += n

    return sum_ofnumbers

print(sum_oflist([1,2,-8]))
```

Solution for Exercise 6

9 days

We've come to the end of the chapter on variables and types. Remember, practice makes perfect. Therefore, you must master all the variables and data types and use the appropriate data types when declaring variables to develop efficient Python programs.

Chapter 4

Python Operators

Programming Operators are symbols you use to tell the interpreter to perform specific operations such as mathematical operations. These operations can range from mathematical to relational or even to logical operations. The Python language interpreter has rich inbuilt operators grouped into the following categories:

- Arithmetic Operators
- Relational Operators
- Logical Operators
- Bitwise Operators
- Assignment Operators

Let's dive in and learn how to use these operators.

#1: Arithmetic Operators

These operators perform arithmetic operations. Here are examples of Python's arithmetic operators and their basic functions:

- +. It adds two operands. For instance, if A=300 and B=100, then A+B gives 400 as the output.
- -. It subtracts the second operand from the first operand. For example, if A=30 0 and B=100, then A - B yields 200 as the output.
- *. It multiplies two or more operands. For example, if A=50 and B=20, then A*B produces 1000 as an output.

- /. It divides the first operand by the second operand. For example, if A=300 and B=200 then, A/B produces 1.5 as an output.
- %. It is a modulus operator; it displays the remainder of a number after performing an integer division. If A=8 and B=3, then A % B yields 2 as the output.
- ++. It increases an integer value by one. For instance, if A=10, then A++ produces 11.
- - -. It is the decrement operator. For example, if A=50, then A- - produces 49.

#2: Relational Operators

Relational operators perform comparisons between two or more operands. Here are examples of relational operators and their functions:

- ==. It checks whether the values of the two operands are equal or not. If they are equal, then condition becomes true; otherwise, it is false. For instance, A==B is only true if A=50 and B=50.
- !=. It compares the values of the two operands to find out whether they are equal or not. For instance, A! =B is false if A=50 and B=50.
- >. It verifies whether the value of the left operand is greater than the value of the operand on the right-hand side.
- <. It verifies whether the value of the left operand is less than the value of the operand on the right-hand side.
- >=. It verifies whether the value of the left operand is greater than or equal to the value of the operand on the right-hand side.
- <=.It checks whether the value of the left operand is less than or equal to the value of the operand on the right-hand side.

#3: Logical Operators

Logical operators are used with the Boolean or logical values. Below are examples of logical operators and their functions:

- && (the logical AND operator). If both the operands are not equal to zero, then the condition is true. Otherwise, the condition is false.
- || (the logical OR operator). If any of two operands is not equal to zero, then the output is true.
- ! (The Logical NOT Operator). It reverses the logical state of the initial operand.

#4: Bitwise Operators

The bitwise operators perform bit-by-bit operations in Python programming. Here are examples of Python's bitwise operators and their functions:

- & (The binary AND operator). It copies a bit to the result if it exists in both the operands.
- | (The binary OR operator). It's used to copy a bit if it exists in either of the operands.
- ^ (The binary XOR operator). It's used to copy the bit if it is set in only one operand and not both the operators.
- << (the binary left shift operator). It moves the left side by a number of bits that are specified by the right operand.

- >>(the binary right shift operator). It is used to move the right side by some bits that are specified by the right operand.

#5: Assignment Operators

Below are examples of assignment operators and their uses:

- =. It assigns values of the right side operands to the left side operand.
- +=. It adds the right operand to left operand and assigns the output to the left operand.
- -=. It subtracts the right operand to left operand and assigns the output to the left operand.
- *=. It multiplies the right operand and left operand and assigns the output to the left operand.
- /=. It divides the right operand and left operand and assigns the output to the left operand.

Ready for an exercise?

Good. Here you go:

Open the Python shell and copy/paste the Python code below, making sure to include every letter and symbol correctly. Press the Enter key to execute the file when you're done.

Python Code:

```
import sys
```

```
def main ():

main()

{

a = 10

d = 10

b = "This Program demonstrates Python Operators."

e = "This Program demonstrates Python Operators."

c = [1, 2, 3]

f = [1,2,3]

print (a is not d)

print (b is e)

Print(c is f)

}
```

What do you see?

Here is one more test.

Python code:

```
x = 10
```

```
n= 12

print ("x > n  is", x>n)

print("x < n  is", x<n)

print("x == n is", x==n)

print("x != n is",x!=n)

print("x >= n is",x>=n)

print("x <= n is",x<=n)
```

Ready for exercises?

Chapter 4 – Fun Exercises

Exercise 7

Write a Python program that checks to verify whether a specified value is contained in a group of data values. For instance, if the test data is [1, 20, 30, 4] and the specified value is 20, then the program should return true and if the test data is [1, 20, 30, 4] and the specified value is 23, then the program should return false.

Exercise 8

Write a Python program to add three given integers. However, if two integer values are equal, then their equal sum will be set to zero.

Solution for Exercise 7

```
import sys

def main ():

main ()

{

def is_ingroup_member(group_data, v):

    for value in group_data:

        if v == value:

            return True

        return False

print(is_ingroup_member([100, 70, 56, 73], 70))

print(is_ingroup_member([76, 81, 65], 7))

}
```

Solution for Exercise 8

```
import sys

def main ():

main ()

{

def sum(a, b, c):

    if a == b or b == c or a==c:

        sum = 0

    else:

        sum = a + b + c

    return sum

print(sum(20, 2, 4))

print(sum(30, 20, 20))

print(sum(40, 40, 40))

print(sum(10, 20, 30))

}
```

We've come to the end of Python operators. You're on your way to becoming a Python guru! Keep up the good work.

Chapter 5

Decision Making and Repetition Structures

The process of decision making in any programming language is certainly necessary to control the flow of the program. Besides allowing you to control the flow of the program, you'll also make decisions based on the user inputs or the results of the processing actions. These decisions are solely based on principles of logic and the relational operators.

For example, if you want to compare two or more variables to determine which one is larger, then you'll be forced to use the relational operators. On the other hand, repetition structures are necessary to specify the processes and instructions that are repetitive. This means that some actions have to be processed until a certain condition has been met. This has two main advantages.

First, you'll be in a position to use your variables in an efficient manner. As I have mentioned earlier, data management is crucial for the successful development of efficient programs. Therefore, instead of declaring so many variables in a code, a repetition structure can be designed to deal with that. By doing so, you'll be minimizing the memory use, which will lead to efficient programs.

Second, and finally, you'll be in a position to organize program statements that are repetitive into a single block based on specific conditions. This will help you to maintain your Python code in a manner that promotes debugging and testing. Basically, there are 5 decision structures you should be aware of in Python programming. These are:

- If...else statement(s)
- For Loop
- While Loop
- Break and Continue
- Pass

So, let's dive in and find out these decision-making structures.

#1: If...else

The simplest if ... statement in Python programming language has the following syntax:

If Boolean expression:

Statement 1

Statement 2

...

Statement n

From the syntax, you should note that the body of the if ... else statement should always be specified by the indentation. This should start with the first un-indented line marks the end of the statement. If you're using an advanced text editor such as the Python IDLE, you shouldn't worry because that will be well taken care of.

When using if ... else statement, the non-zeroed values are interpreted as true while null and zero are will be interpreted as false.

Below is an illustration of Python code that tests if the average is greater than or equal to 70 and displays grade "A."

---

mynumber = float(input("Enter any number from the Keyboard: "))

```
if number > 70:

    print ("The grade is A")
```

The if ... else statement will only be executed when the Boolean expression is true. In the above example, the program will only display grade A if the mynumber is greater than 7. If mynumber is less than 70, then the statement will be skipped.

In some instance, if statement may be followed by an else statement that is optional. When there's optional if ... else statement, then the optional statement will be executed only when the Boolean expression returns false. Below is the syntax:

```
If Boolean expression:

Statement 1

Statement 2

...

Statement n

Else:

Statement 1

Statement 2

...
```

Statement n

In this case, the program will evaluate the Boolean expression and execute the body statements only when test condition is true. However, if the Boolean condition is False, then the body of the else will be executed. Here's an example:

```
mynumber = float (input ("Enter any positive number from the Keyboard: "))

if mynumber > 50:

print ("Passed")

else:
```

print ("Failed")If you want to specify multiple expressions, then you must use the elif statement, which is synonymous with else if nested statements in other languages. If the Boolean condition is false, then the program will check the Boolean condition of the next elif block of statements and the process goes on.

Here's illustration of Python code that demonstrates the elif:

```
mynumber = float(input("Type any number from the Keyboard: "))

if mynumber > 0:

print ("The number you have entered is positive number")
```

```
elif mynumber == 0:

print("The number you've entered is Zero"):

else:

print ("The number you have entered is a negative number")
```

Ready for another test?

Well, open the Python shell and copy/paste the Python code below. Make sure to include every letter and symbol correctly. When you're done, execute the file.

Python Code:

```
import sys

def main ():

main()

{

if average>=70:

grade="A."

elif average>=60:

grade=" B."

elif average>=50:
```

```
grade=" C."

elif average>=40:

grade=" D."

else:

grade=" F."

}
```

#2: For Loop

The for loop iterates over a sequence that may have different data types such as the list, tuple, and string. It can also iterate any other objects that may be defined in Python. Below is the syntax for the for loop:

```
for val in sequence:

Statement 1

Statement 2

...

Statement n
```

In the syntax above, Val defines the variable that takes the value of the item that's contained in the sequence for each of the iterative process. The looping process will continue as long as the last item in the sequence has not been reached. Below is an example of the Python code that shows how the sum of all numbers stored in a list can be obtained:

```
mynumber = [10,20,30,40,50,60,70,80,90,100]

sum = 0

for val in numbers:

sum = sum + val

print ("The sum of 10 numbers in your list is", sum)
```

#3: While Loop

The while loop loops over a block of statements only if the Boolean expression is true. Here's the syntax of the Python's while Loop:

```
while Boolean expression:

Statement 1

Statement 2

...

Statement n
```

The Boolean expression is evaluated first. If the condition is true, the program statements in the body of the loop will be executed. After the first iteration, the Boolean condition is checked again. This process will continue until the Boolean expression evaluates to false.

Below is an example of the Python code that prompts a user to enter n numbers from the Keyboard and sums them:

```
x = int (input ("Enter any positive number n :"))

total = 0

index = 1

while index <= n:

    sum = total+ index

    index = index+1

print ("The sum of the first n numbers is:", total)
```

#4: Break and Continue

There are some instances when you just want to end the current loop, for loop and the while loop, or even the whole loop without first executing the Boolean expression. In this case, the break and continue statements changes the flow of a normal loop in Python.

When you break a loop using the break statement, control of the program will be transferred to the program statements that are placed after the body of the loop. However, if the statement that's being executed is inside the nested loop, then the break statement will end the innermost loop. Below is the syntax for break statement:

```
break
```

Below is an example of a Python code that uses the break statement:

```
for val in "Python Programming Comprehensive Guide For Programmers":

if val == "e":

break

print(val)

print("The program has reached the end of the string")
```

The continue statement is used to skip the rest of the code that is inside the loop for the current iteration only. In such a case, the loop will not end but will continue with the next loop instruction. The syntax for continue is:

```
continue
```

Here's an example of code that uses the continue statement in Python:

```
for val in "Python Programming Comprehensive Guide For
Programmers":

 if val == "e":

continue

print(val)

print("The program has reached the end of the string")
```

#5: Pass

The pass statement is always treated as the null statement. Why is the pass statement important? Well, the Python interpreter usually ignores the comments, but the past statements have to be executed. However, nothing will happen when the pass statement has been executed. In other words, the pass statement will act as the placeholder. For example, if you have a loop that hasn't been implemented, but you want to implement in the future, then you can use the pass statement.

Below is an example:

```
def function(args):

pass

class BankingSystem:

pass
```

Let's see how you're fairing on with the exercises.

Chapter 5 – Fun Exercises

Exercise 9

Write a Python program that counts the number of even and odd numbers in a sequence of numbers. For instance if the sample sequence is: [1,2,3,4,5,6,7,8,9,10,11] then the expected output will be:

Number of even numbers: 5

Number of odd numbers: 6

Exercise 10

Write a Python program that creates a multiplication table from 1 to 10 of an input number. For instance if the input number is 8, then the expected output will be

Input a number: 68

8 x 1 = 8

8 x 2 = 16

8 x 3 = 24

8 x 4 = 32

8 x 5 = 40

8 x 6 = 48

8 x 7 =56

8 x 8 = 64

8 x 9 = 72

8 x 10 = 80

Solution for Exercise 9

```
import sys

def main ():

main ()

{

mynumber = (1, 2, 3, 4, 5, 6, 7, 8, 9,10,11)

count_ofoddnumbers = 0

count_ofevennumbers = 0

for index in mynumber:

    if not index % 2:

count_ofevennumbers +=1

    else:

        count_ofoddnumbers +=1

print("The number of even numbers are :",
count_ofevennumbers)

print(The number of odd numbers are:", count_ofoddnumbers)

}
```

```
import sys

def main ():

main ()

{

n = int(input("Input a number:"))  # We're using the for loop to
iterate 10 times

for index in range(1,11):

   print(n, "x",index, "=",n*index)

}
```

There you have it. Next up, we explore Python functions and modules.

Chapter 6

Python Functions and Modules

In this chapter, we explore the Python functions and modules. By the end of this chapter, you will be in a position to define and use your own Python functions and modules. But first, what exactly are functions and modules?

A function can be conceived as procedures or any section of the program that is independent of the main program that produces an output. The function can help to map zero or more input arguments and produce an output. The main objective of designing a function in a Python code is to assist place program statements into a block that can perform related tasks.

On the other hand, a module objects that has arbitrarily named attributes bind a particular reference. In other words, a module is a file that consists of Python code that breaks down the whole program into manageable units. The whole essence of having modules is to promote modularization, where the program is broken down to allow for easier debugging and testing. A module can have functions and classes, together with its own variables.

What about functions?

Functions provide every useful insight whenever you want to create constructs that organize your code. Any program that lacks functions may be difficult to manage because it can be confusing. Debugging such programs may not be a walk in the park. In addition, having functions in your program makes the code reusable.

Here's syntax of python functions:

```
def name_of_the_function (parameters):

Statement 1

Statement 2

...

Statement n
```

Below are the main components to note about the function:

- Any function you declare must start with keyword "def", which marks the start of the function header.
- The keyword "def" must be followed by the name of the function you're developing. The name of the function should follow the conventional rules when naming identifiers.
- The arguments or parameters that are passed to the function are optional.
- The colon (:) marks the end of function header.
- The function body will be composed of one or more valid program statements.
- The optional return statement returns a value for the function.

Below is an illustration of how you can specify a function in Python:

```
def greetings(myname):

print("Hello!" "+myname + ". Good evening! Are you OK?")
```

Calling a function

When you define a function, you can call it from any other function, any program, or even from the Python shell. If you want to call a function, simply type the name of the function and specify the appropriate parameters. Below is an example of a Python code that calls the function that we had declared in our previous section.

```
greeting("Ronald Olsen")
```

Below is the output of the program:

```
Hello! Ronald Olsen. Good evening! Are you OK?
```

Return values

In some instances, you may want to exit from the function and return to the location in the program from where it was called. The return statement helps programmers to exit from a function and go back to program location where the function was called. Below is the syntax of the return statement:

```
return [expression_list]
```

The return statement may or may not contain expressions. If it contains the expression list, then the list will be evaluated to find out which value to return. If there is no expression list in the statement, then the function will return a null object. Below is an illustration:

```
def absolute_value_of_a_number(mynumber):

  if mynumber >= 10:

    return mynumber
```

```
else:

    return -mynumber

print(absolute_value_of_a_number(200))

print(absolute_value_of_a_number (-500))
```

Pass by reference and pass by value

All the function arguments (parameters) in Python language are passed by reference. What does this mean? It simply means that the function output and its definition are tied together. If you try to alter one value of a parameter within the function, then the change will also be reflected back in the calling function.

Take a look at the following function:

```
def change_me( mylist ): # This declares a function with the name change_me with mylist as arguments
```

Now, suppose we want to append some data on the list. We will use the following statement:

```
mylist. Append ([1, 2, 3, 4])
```

To display the contents of the list, we have to call the function by its name as follows:

```
print ("The values contained inside the function are:", mylist)
```

```
return
```

We can also call the function as follows:

```
mylist = [40,10,20,50]

change_me (mylist)
```

If we want to display the contents of the list, we'll now use the following statement (call by reference, because the calling function has also been changed).

```
print ("The values outside the function are:", mylist)
```

Types of Functions

There are two basic categories of functions in Python:

- Built-in functions
- User-defined functions

Let's jump in and find out the distinctions between built-in and user-defined functions.

#1: Built-in functions

These are functions that have already been built and ported into the Python. For instance, functions such as print (), input (), etc., that we've been using so far in our illustrations,are examples of Python built-in functions. Other examples of Python functions are: abs(), divmod(), open(), staticmethod(), all(), enumerate(), int(), ord(), str(), any(), eval(), isinstance(), pow(), sum(), basestring(), execfile(),issubclass(), bin(), file(), iter(), property(), tuple(), bool(), filter(), len(), etc.

Let's examine the special class of built-in functions—the input and output functions.

#1: Input functions

Here are examples of input functions:

    a. The raw_input () Function

The raw_input ([prompt]) function is used to read one line from the standard input and returns it as a string to be stored in the main memory. Here's an illustration:

```
mystring = raw_input("Enter the data:")

print ("Received input is: ", mystring)
```

    b. The input Function

The input ([prompt]) function is similar to a raw_input function, except that it assumes that the input is a valid Python expression. Here's an illustration:

```
mystring = input("Enter the value of your input: ");

print ("Received input is:", mystring)
```

    c. The open Function

This function is used to open a file. It creates a file object that can be utilized to call other support methods associated with it. Here's the syntax for the function.

```
file object = open (file_name , access_mode)
```

#2: Output functions

Below are examples of Python's output functions:

a. Print () function

It's used to display a message on the computer screen. Here's an example:

```
a = "3000"

b = "2000"

print (x + y)

print int(x) + int(y)
```

#2: User-defined functions

These are functions that are specified by users. The user defined functions are important because of the following reasons:

- They allow you to break down a large code into small segments that make your program easier to understand and debug.

- If you're working on a very large project, then the user-defined functions can help you to divide the workload into different functions.

Below is an example of a user-defined function in action...

```
def absolute_value_of_a_number(mynumber):

  if mynumber >= 10:

    return mynumber

  else:

    return -mynumber

print(absolute_value_of_a_number(200))

print(absolute_value_of_a_number (-500))
```

Python Modules

Python modules are essentially reusable libraries of code that can be imported and used in a program. Python interpreter is shipped with many standard library modules. The modules are imported using the import statement. Here's an example:

```
Import module_name
```

Here's an illustration:

```
import time
```

```
print time.asctime()
```

The above Python code imports the time module and calls the function, asctime, which returns the current time as a string. The above code can also be specified as follows:

```
from time import asctime

asctime()
```

In the example above, we've imported the time function and used the asctime from the time module.

Writing modules

Writing Python modules is pretty simple. To create your own module, simply create a new ".py" file with the module name. For instance, the code below can be converted into a module if it's saved with a ".py" file extension:

```
import sys

def main ():

main()

{

a = 10

d = 10
```

```
b = "This Program demonstrates Python Operators."

e = "This Program demonstrates Python Operators."

c = [1, 2, 3]

f = [1,2,3]

print (a is not d)

print (b is e)

Print(c is f)

}
```

If the above file is saved as mymodule.py, then it can be imported and used in a new code as follows:

```
Import mymodule
```

Don't give up on practicing. By adhering to the rules of Python functions and modules that you've learned in this chapter, you'll be on your way to becoming a professional Python programmer!

Chapter 6 – Fun Exercises

Exercise 11

Write a Python function that computes the factorial of a number of a non-negative integer. The function should accept the number as an argument and display the output.

Exercise 12

Write a Python function which takes any number as a parameter and checks to confirm whether the number is a prime number or not. Note that a prime number any natural number that is greater than 1 and no positive divisors other than 1 and itself.

Solution for Exercise 11

```
import sys

def main ():

main ()

{

def factorial(m):

    if m == 0:

        return 1

    else:

        return m * factorial(m-1)

n=int(input("Enter a number to compute its factorial :"))

print(factorial(m))

}
```

Solution for Exercise 12

```python
def test_theprimenumber(m):

    if (m==1):

        return False

    elif (m==2):

        return True;

    else:

        for x in range(2,m):

            if(m % x==0):

                return False

        return True

print(test_theprimenumber (12))
```

Chapter 7

Python Classes

Even before we start to write the actual Python programs using classes, we need to mention that Python language is an object-oriented programming language. Therefore, it follows all the concepts of object-oriented programming languages. As a Python programmer, you should be familiar with the basic concepts of object-oriented programming and its application in Python programming.

Of course, the most important concepts in any object-oriented programming language are the class and the object. Therefore, to understand why Python language is an object-oriented programming language we need to start by defining classes and objects. So, what is a class?

What is a class?

To define a class, let me use the concept of groupings to help you understand it. Our brains can help us to group certain features. For instance, we know that lions, human beings, cats, and dogs all belong to animals. In this case, animals are groupings of lions, human beings, cats, and dogs. We can, therefore, say that lions, human beings, cats, and dogs belong to a class of animals.

But how does the brain allow us to arrive at this conclusion? It's because we know that all animals have certain characteristics that you can't find in plants. In other words, our brain creates abstractions and thinks hierarchically based on the characteristics we have. In programming, the functions can help us to abstract a sequence of operations that we would like to apply to members of the same class. But we also need to abstract groupings of data that may be complex. That's where the concept of classes comes in.

Consider a social network site such as Facebook or Twitter. Which data are you going to record for each member in the social media system? You must define a class to help you manage such a system. A class will essentially be an extensible program code template that you'll use to for creating objects—

those members that have similar characteristics. The class will allow you provide initial values for different states (member variables) and implementations for the various behaviors in the system.

In other words, a class will serve as a template for creating, or instantiating, specific objects within the program. Although each object is created from a single class, a single class can be used to create multiple objects. In Python programming, classes are specified using the following syntax:

```
class name_of_the_class[(expr[,expr]*)]:

class members and methods
```

Any class you create must start with the keyword "class" followed by a name (name_of_the_class). The class must be defined based on the attributes it supports. The class definition is an executable statement and because of this, it can be used wherever an executable statement occurs in a Python code. When it's executed, each expression is evaluated and within a class where the class members and methods are executed in the new local namespace. Basically, the class statements in the body of the class are assignments and the function definitions. After execution class statements, the class name is bound to the new class in the outer, which is the calling namespace, and the new namespace of the class definition is automatically associated with the class object.

Consider the code below:

```
Class Person:  # class definition

person_name=""

Age=0

Friends = []
```

The above code creates a class called Person and associates the characteristics of each person using the methods person_name, age, and friends. Note that you can define any function within the class and set the variables to use. For instance, you could design a function that displays the age of a person. In the above example, the variables have been set outside the class.

Objects

Once you define a class, you can begin to create instances of it. Whatever you create will be called instance objects. I know you may be wondering, "What are objects?"

In the broadest term, an object can be regarded as a thing, tangible or intangible, that you can imagine. Any program that's written in object-oriented programming style must consist of interacting objects. Take the case of banking accounts program. You can specify different bank accounts ranging from current, savings, or fixed deposit accounts.

These accounts will be instances of objects that have been derived from the class of bank accounts. Any object you instantiate must have data and the operations that manipulate the data. For instance, the savings account may contain the account number, the account holder's details (name, phone number, e-mail address, etc.), date opened, the initial balance, current balance, and operation such as deposits and transfers.

In our earlier code, we can instantiate the objects of the class Person using the example code below:

```
# main

Ronald = Person ()    # this creates a Person object with
person_name="" and age=0

 print Ronald. Age    # prints 0

Ronald. Age=34

Ronald.name="Ronald Olsen"
```

Inheritance

Inheritance is a powerful feature in any object-oriented programming. Basically, inheritance is the act of creating a new class with little or no modifications from an already defined class. The new class will be called the derived, or child, class, and the one from which it has inherited from is called the base class. The derived class inherits all the features from the base class while adding new features to it. This is the basis of code reuse in a programming language.

Below is the syntax of the inheritance in Python:

```
class DerivedClass(BaseClass):

body_of_derived_class
```

To demonstrate the use of inheritance, look at the example below:

```
class Polygon:

   def __init__ (self, no_of_sides):

      self.n = no_of_sides_polygon

      self.sides = [0 for index in range (no_of_sides_polygon)]

 def inputSides(self):

      self.sides = [double (input ("Enter side"+str (index+1) + ":"))
for index in range (self.n)]

   def dispSides(self):

      for index in range(self.n):
```

```
print("Side",index+1, "is",self.sides[index])
```

The above class has data attributes that stores the number of sides, n, and size of each side as a list which are sides. The method inputSides () takes in the magnitude of each side of the polygon while the method dispSides () displays the values.

Let's say you want to define a triangle class. We all know that a triangle is a polygon with 3 sides. Therefore, we can define it as a class called Triangle that inherits from the Polygon class. After inheritance, all the attributes which were available in class Polygon will be available in the new class Triangle.

Here's an illustration:

```
class Triangle(Polygon):

  def _init_(self):

    Polygon._init_ (self, 3)

  def find_the_Area (self):

    x, y, z = self.sides

 # calculate the perimeter of the Triangle

    s = (x + y + z)

    area = (s*(s-x)*(s-y)*(s-z)) ** 0.5

    print( "The area of the triangle is %0.2f" %area)
```

From the above example, we can see that even though we didn't specify the methods such as inputSides () or dispSides () for class Triangle, you'll still be in a position to use them. This means that if any attribute is not found within the class, the search proceeds to the base class. This process repeats recursively.

Chapter 7 – Fun Exercises

Exercise 13

Write a Python program that finds a pair of elements—indices of two numbers—from a given array where the sum equals a specific target number.

Exercise 14

Write a Python class that finds the three elements that sum to zero from a set of m real numbers.

Solution for Exercise 13

```
class myclass:

    def twoSum_function(self, num, target):

        lookup = {}

        for index, num in enumerate(num):

            if target - num in lookup:

                return (lookup[target - num] + 1, index + 1)

            lookup[num] = index

print("index1=%d, index2=%d" % myclass ().twoSum_function
((20,10,10,70,100,60,70),40))
```

Solution for Exercise 14

```
class myclass:

 def three_Sum(self, num):

    num, result, index = sorted(num), [], 0

    while index < len(num) - 2:

       j, k = index + 1, len(num) - 1

       while j < k:

          if num[index] + num[j] + num[k] < 0:

             j += 1

          elif num[i] + num[j] + num[k] > 0:

             k -= 1

          else:

             result. Append ([num[index], num[j], num[k]])

             j, k = j + 1, k - 1

             while j < k and num[j] == num[j - 1]:

                j += 1

             while j < k and num[k] == num[k + 1]:

                k -= 1
```

555

```
            index += 1

        while index < len(num) - 2 and num[i] == num[index - 1]:

            index += 1

        return result

print(myclass().three_Sum([5, 10, 7, 9, 2, 4, 8, 10]))
```

Chapter 8

Error Handling and Exceptions

This chapter explores mechanisms for error handling and exceptions. Until now, we haven't dealt with the errors. Therefore, if you encountered any errors in the previous examples, you may not have had an idea on how to deal with them. Are you ready?

There are two main categories of programming errors. These are:

- Syntax errors
- Semantic errors

Let's dive in and explore the differences between these errors.

#1: Syntax errors

Syntax errors, sometimes called the parsing errors, are errors that emanate from the source code of the program. Because computer programs must strictly adhere to grammar and the structure of the program, any aspects of the code that don't conform to the syntax will generate a syntax error. For instance, if you to run the code below, you'll encounter a syntax error:

```
import sys

def main ():

main()

{

a = =10

d = 10

b == "This Program demonstrates Python Operators."

e == "This Program demonstrates Python Operators."

c == [1, 2, 3]

f == [1,2,3]

print (a is not d)
```

```
print (b is e)

Print(c is f)

}
```

In the above example, the error is caused by the assignment operators (==) that have been used with variables b, e, and c.

#2: Semantic errors

Semantic errors are those errors that arise from the compiler understanding and executing code but not according to the programmer's dictates. If there is a semantic error in a program, the program will run successfully because the syntax is correct; however, the program will not perform what it was intended to. It will perform something else. Identifying the semantic errors can be difficult because it requires you to work backward by re-looking at the output of the program.

Let's examine the common errors you'll encounter while programming in Python.

#1: Null error

Null errors in a Python program results from dereferencing a null pointer. The Null errors are usually the result of one or more program assumptions that are being violated in a Python program. This can result from software reliability issues. The null pointer errors take place when a pointer that has a null value is used as though it pointed to a valid memory area.

For instance, the code below will result in a null error:

```
if (pointer1 != NULL) {

free(pointer1)

pointer1 = NULL;

}
```

#2: ZeroDivision Error

The ZeroDivision error occurs when the second argument of the division operation or modulo operation is zero.

#3: FileNotFound Error

The FileNotFound Error occurs when you try to open a file that's not defined. To correct this, you have to use the "isfile" method.

Take a look at the Python code below:

```
import os

if ( not os.path.isfile(_Python)):

    print ("There's an error: %s file not found",% error)

else:

    print ("Setting up the environment %s ..."% Python)
```

Exceptions

Even if a program statement or expression is syntactically correct, it can generate an error when an attempt is made to run it. The errors detected during the execution of the program are called exceptions. Exceptions are not unconditionally fatal if they are handled properly.

Handling Exceptions

Exception handling is the act of responding to the occurrence that occurs during the computation of exceptions. This requires changing the normal execution flow of the program. This must be provided by very specialized programming language constructs. In Python language, it is possible to write programs that handle the selected exceptions.

The following are examples of mechanisms of handling exceptions:

#1: Try Catch Exception

Take a look at the example below:

```
while True:

try:

a = int (input ("Please enter a positive number: "))

break

except ValueError:

print("Oops!  That was not a valid number.  Please Try again
later")
```

The above code asks the user for an input that is a valid integer. But the program allows the user to interrupt the flow of the program. The user generated interruption will be signaled by the keyboard. The try statement in the above code works as follows:

- First, the try clause and the statements between the try and except keywords will be executed.
- If there's no exception then except clause will be skipped and running of the try statement will be completed.
- If an exception occurs during the execution of the try clause, the rest of the clause statements will be skipped. If the type matches the exception that's named after

except keyword, then except clause will be executed after the try statement.

The try statement can have more than one except clause that specifies handlers for the different exceptions. In any exception, at most one handler will be executed. The handlers can only handle exceptions that occur in the corresponding try clause. An except clause can have multiple exception statements within the same try statement. Here's an example:

```
class myclass(Exception):

 pass

class another_class(myclass):

 pass

class D(another_class):

pass

for index in [myclass, another_class, D]:

  try:

    raise index()

  except D:

    print("D")
```

```
except another_class:

  print("another_class")

except myclass:

  print("myclass")
```

Chapter 9

Testing Your Code

This chapter explains the process of testing your Python code after you've completed the coding process. By the end of the chapter, you'll be familiar with all the concepts regarding software testing and how unit and integration testing are conducted. Why is testing an important component of software development process?

Before you present your software to the client, you have to make sure all the customer's concerns have been well taken care of. It's pointless to spend so much time developing a program that will be rejected by the customer. Therefore, as a programmer, it is crucial to test all the important aspects of your software to ensure it's not only running correctly but it has also addressed your client's concerns.

By testing the software, you'll be in a position to identify any mistakes or errors and correct them before handing over the software to the customer. The process of testing the software can occur at various stages of software development. The process shouldn't be a one-off time. It can get repeated at various stages until the final unit of the program is completed.

Types and levels of testing

Here are types and levels of testing:

- White box testing
- Black box testing
- Unit testing
- Integration testing
- Regression testing
- Alpha testing
- Beta testing

Let's examine these testing strategies.

#1: White Box Testing

In this type of testing, you have to access the source code of the software you want to test. This means that you have to gain a complete access and control of the source code. You must be knowledgeable about the programming language that has been used to implement the source code. The main objective of white box testing is to derive the test data from the program logic code so that any inconsistencies that are noted are corrected.

#2: Black Box Testing

Black box testing can also be referred to as functional testing. Unlike the white box testing, where the source code is examined for inconsistencies, black box testing allows the programmer to access the output or outcome of the code to confirm whether the developed software is addressing the customer concerns. The final software product has to behave in a manner that satisfies the client.

#3: Unit Testing

In unit testing, each module or function of the software is conducted to ensure it's working correctly according to the requirement specifications. This level of testing is conducted to ensure of every module in the program. It's usually done by programmers who are writing the test cases for each of the scenarios in the modules of the software.

#4: Regression testing

You are aware that the development of software may not be a discrete affair where the program development isn't subjected to continuous changes. In a typical programming environment, the program you'll be developing will be subjected to continuous changes dictated by the clients. Therefore, you should always ensure that each change made to the system is tested to ensure it has satisfied your client.

As you manage the changes in the software, you should ensure that the existing software system is essentially the one your clients proposed. That is why regression testing is necessary. The main objective of regression testing is to allow your software remain intact even after incorporating the changes suggested by your clients.

#5: Integration testing

By unit testing for every module, the process of integration testing is made simpler. When you correct the mistakes or bugs in every module, integration testing will become easier because it entails incorporating all the modules that have been thoroughly tested. Integration testing covers all the aspects of the modules in the program.

Integration testing is best suited to iterative software process models as it saves time in the long run and helps to keep the project to acceptable budget. This is because iterative process models allow for more feedback from the customer. When the customer is more involved in the testing stages, there are higher chances of the software being acceptable in the long run.

#6: Alpha Testing

The bottom line in any software development is to test the software and release it to customers. The testing approaches we've examined earlier looks at testing from the point of view of requirements and customer needs. This means that testing is being conducted to ascertain that it is conforming to customer requirements and needs.

However, the final testing is still necessary before the product is released to customers. Alpha testing is software testing that is conducted before the software system is released to the client. It involves both the white box and black box testing. Therefore, you'll be required to conduct the testing at two phases: white box and black box testing.

#7: Beta Testing

Beta testing is carried out to ensure the validity of the software is guaranteed. It takes place in the alpha testing. Essentially, the software product is released to a set of users and feedback is generated from them to ensure the validity of the program. Therefore, beta testing can be conceived as testing that is carried out by a group of end users.

Having discussed the different types of testing strategies, let's now focus on the testing process itself.

Testing process

Before embarking on testing, it's important to communicate to all the developers who have been involved in the software. They may not necessarily be programmers but you have to ensure the client, the system analysts, programmers, and database developers have been involved. The testing strategies can be conducted in parallel if you're worried about the delivery time of the software.

Next, you have to design a test plan. I am now sure you're asking, "What does a test plan look like?"

Test plan

Well, a test plan is any strategy you have concerning how you would like to proceed with the testing process. It's the guide that will be used throughout the testing process. It will contain information such as:

- Development environment of the developed software.
- The hardware requirements
- The operating system
- The scope of the software
- The limitation of testing
- The testing type to be conducted.

Next up, you'll proceed to the actual testing, which involves designing the test case. But before you proceed to actual testing, you have to be at peace with all the requirements of the test plan.

Test case

A test case documents test scenario that you'll prepare to conduct the different levels of testing. It must have the following components:

- A set of test data
- The pre-conditions
- The expected results
- The post conditions

The report that is generated must factor in the errors or defects that have been identified between expected outcome and actual output in every module. The test case report is then sent to developers for program refinement.

PYTHON CHEAT SHEET

Python Basics

Use proper indentation. Your code will fail to run if whitespace is present.

Use # for comments. E.g. #This is a comment.

Basic Python Logics

If:

```
If condition:

        #execute statements if condition is true

elif condition 2

        # execute statements if condition 2 is true

else:

        # execute statements if both conditions are false
```

While:

```
While condition:

        #keep running statements until condition is false
```

For:

```
For value in sequence:

    #execute statements for each member of sequence

    #for example, each item in a list, etc.
```

Python Variables and Data Types

String:

String is a sequence of characters used to store text.

String creation:

```
mystring = "Learn Python!"
mystring = 'Learn Python!'
```

String accessing:

```
mystring[6]           returns 'P'
```

String splitting:

```
mystring.split(' ')    returns ['Learn','Python!']
mystring.split('h')    returns ['Learn Pyt', 'on!']
```

String joining:

```
words = ['This', "is", 'weird', 'but', 'it', "works!"]

''.join(words)          returns "Thisisweirdbutitworks!"

' '.join(words)         returns "This is weird but it works!"

'COOL'.join(words)   returns
"ThisCOOLisCOOLweirdCOOLbutCOOLitCOOLworks!"
```

String formatting:

```
mystring = "kindly help to review"
print "Please %s!"%mystring        returns "Please kindly help to
review!"
```

Tuples:

A tuple consists of values separated by commas. They are often used to manage ordered pairs and returning multiple values from a function.

Tuple creation:

```
emptyTuple = ()
singleItemTuple = ("one",)   #note the comma
mytuple = 20, 17, 't'
mytuple = (20, 17, 't')
```

Tuple accessing:

```
mytuple[0]     returns 20
```

Dictionaries:

A dictionary is a set of key value pairs. All keys in a dictionary are unique.

Dictionary creation:

```
myemptydictionary = {}
mydictionary = {"name": "Ronald Olsen", "code":722848386,
"dept": "IT"}
```

Dictionary accessing:

```
mydictionary['name']          returns Ronald Olsen
```

Dictionary deleting:

```
del mydictionary['code']
```

Dictionary finding:

```
mydictionary.has_key('code')      returns false
mydictionary.keys()               returns ['name','dept']
mydictionary.items()              returns [('name','Ronald
Olsen'),('dept','IT')]
'dept' in mydictionary            returns true
'phone number' in mydictionary    returns false
```

Python List Manipulation

List creation:

```
mylist = ['virgo',1,'taurus','capricorn',3]
```

List accessing:

```
mylist[0]       returns virgo
```

List slicing:

```
mylist[1:3]    returns [1,'taurus']
mylist[2:]     returns ['taurus','capricorn',3]
mylist[:2]     returns ['virgo',1]
mylist[2:-1]   returns ['taurus','capricorn']
```

List length:

```
len(mylist)    returns 5
```

List sort:

```
Mylist.sort()   #no return value
        [1,3,'capricorn','taurus','virgo']
```

List add:

```
mylist.append(21)    #[1,3,'capricorn','taurus','virgo',21]
```

List return & remove:

```
mylist.pop()   returns 21     #[1,3,'capricorn','taurus','virgo']
mylist.pop(2)          returns capricorn    #[1,3,'taurus','virgo']
```

List insert:

```
mylist.insert(2,6)                     #[1,3,6,'taurus','virgo']
```

List remove:

```
len(mylist.remove('taurus')          #[1,3,6,'virgo']
```

List concatenation:

```
mylist + [9]    returns [1,3,6,'virgo',9]
```

List finding:

```
"virgo" in mylist       returns true
```

Files Manipulation

Open file:

```
myfile = open("datadirectory/myfilename.txt")
```

Take note of the forward slash. open() function has read only permission.

Access file:

```
myfile.read()                #reads entire file into one string
myfile.readline()                 #reads one line of a file
myfile.readlines()                 #reads entire file into list of
strings, one per line
for eachline in myfile:                 #step through lines in
a file
```

RESOURCES

Web Development

Python Standard Libraries & Package Index– http://www.python.org

Module

Mechanize - http://wwwsearch.sourceforge.net/mechanize/

Framework

Django - https://www.djangoproject.com/

Pylons - http://pylonsproject.org/

Micro-Framework

Flask - http://flask.pocoo.org/

Bottle - http://bottlepy.org/docs/dev/

Software Development

Scons – http://www.scons.org/

Builddot - http://buildbot.net/

Apache Gump – http://gump.apache.org/

Roundup – http://roundup.sourceforge.net/

Advanced Content Management

Plone – https://plone.org/

Django CMS - https://www.django-cms.org/en/

Scientific and Numeric Analysis

SciPy - http://scipy.org/

Panda - http://pandas.pydata.org/

IPython - http://ipython.org/

Desktop GUIs

wxWidgets - https://www.wxpython.org/

Kivy - https://kivy.org/

Qt - https://wiki.qt.io/PySide

Plaform Specific

GTK+ - http://www.pygtk.org/

Home Automation

Home Assistant - https://github.com/home-assistant/home-assistant

OpenHAB - http://www.openhab.org/

Amazing Things To Do with Python

Everyday Life - http://avilpage.com/2014/08/amazing-things-to-do-with-python-in.html

Daily Challenge -

http://interactivepython.org/runestone/static/everyday/index.html

Free Tutorials

https://www.learnpython.org/

https://developers.google.com/edu/python/exercises/basic

http://www.pythonchallenge.com/

Advanced Courses

Advance Python Courses from University of Michigan -

https://goo.gl/XPfw3N

Full Stack Web Development from Hong Kong University of Science and Technology - https://goo.gl/H2mO9R

Intermediate Python Course of Data Analysis and Visualization -

https://goo.gl/2ZZczB

CONCLUSION

I know that programming isn't a walk in the park for most students. Truth be told, I also had the same mentality. But I can guarantee you that this mentality won't get you anywhere. I had to learn the hard way and discard this mentality. That's why I'm a professional Python programmer. You have to take a positive approach and start from some point. I'm glad that you've taken the first step.

The next step is putting in a lot of practice. Remember, the rule of thumb in learning any programming language, Python included, is practice and having a positive attitude. I'm also glad that you've chosen the Python language. There's no doubt about the power of Python programming language. It's a fact that Python programming language has overtaken the most popular object-oriented programming languages such as Java, C++, Perl, and Ruby in recent times.

Do you know that Python is often preferred over other languages such C++ and Java because of 3 things (pseudo-code-like syntax , dynamic typing and has an interpreter) and the cool things is it integrates well with C++.

Therefore, you made the right choice to specialize in Python language. I can assure you that you won't regret it. Besides mastering the core concepts of the language, you're now in a position to learn virtually any object-oriented programming language!

Do you have any questions regarding Python language? Share your concerns with us.

PART II: LEARN PYTHON (ADVANCED) IN 7

DAY AND ACE IT WELL

The Only Book You Need To Start Master and Excel In
Python Programming Now

PREFACE

Learning and coding in Python can be a frustrating affair. However, once you have mastered Python as a valuable skill set, it will provides massive benefits to your personal growth, career progression or open new options for you.

We understand the pain in learning a new programming language. Often, you'll be left in the dust simply because you can't get a hold of a book that understands your pains but I do and this is why my team and I are going to make it a breeze for you with hands on challenges that you could practice right away after each chapter, just like my other popular python programming book "Learn Python in a Day And Master It Well".

Truth be told—the programming environment is changing fast. Really fast! Catching up with the latest buzz can be quite challenging affair.

You may wonder if Python is another programming fad?

In the last couple of decades, Python has emerged as a multi-purpose language for powering web applications, games, machine learning, finance and even natural language processing. Today, Python is powering some of the most important applications in large corporations such as YouTube, Mozilla, Google, Reddit, Facebook, New York Times and Twitter.

What does this mean for programmers?

Good news! It is a skill set in high demand! It means that you have to catch up with the latest features or libraries that Python programming is providing towards fulfilling these important computing areas.

If you've just mastered the basic Python programming concepts, then this book if for you. It will help you shift from a novice Python programmer to an expert Python programmer within a short period of time.

Don't worry if you've never coded in Python. Get hold of our "Learn Python in a Day And Master It Well" and you'll be in a position to begin coding in this important language.

Together with this book, it provides all the information that you need to have to become an advanced Python programmer.

From iterators to generators to descriptors, you'll explore all the important features that Python offers for advanced programmers. And that's not all. You'll also explore some of the Python's powerful data analysis libraries that are making Python bypass R. At the end of each chapter, there are Challenges together with solutions that will test your understand of the concepts covered. It is my hope that you'll grasp all the basics of Python programming that you need to become an advanced programmer.

140

Chapter 1

Introduction

Perhaps you've just completed learning the basics of Python, or maybe you're an experienced programmer with a solid command of C, C++, and Java. So, what next?

Well, after a whirlwind review of programming fundamentals, it's now time to delve deeper into Python's advanced but powerful features that will make you into a proficient programmer ready to take on any challenges. In "Python Programming Comprehensive Guide for Advanced Programmers", we will delve deeper into Python's advanced programming features such as the user-defined classes, the decorators and generators to help you with writing useful web applications.

Besides understanding new features in Python that you didn't cover in fundamentals of Python programming, you'll also learn how to use Python's common libraries to solve difficult programming problems. In particular, you'll explore statistical libraries such as NumPy, Pandas, and Matplotlib that have been shipped with Python and will help you in data analysis and mining.

You'll also learn how to apply and use industry-standard tools for when working within a Python development team, such as that of refactoring, the Git for versioning, the code review and much more. With these tools in mind, you can begin to benchmark, optimize and even test your Python programs for efficient use of memory and CPU.

Fret not, for we are also cognizant of the fact that learning and coding in Python can be frustrating. Despite the massive benefits that Python provides, you can be left in the dust simply because you can't get hold on a book that understands your pains! This very book has been written such that it is easy to understand, hence clearing any hurdles that you may have with regards to understanding Python programming.

That's not all.

At the end of every chapter, there are practical Challenges to test you on the topic that had just been covered. You'll have the chance to practice and compare your solutions with the answers that are provided at the end of the chapter.

Let's dive in.

Chapter 2

Understanding Python

When Guido van Rossum developed the Python programming language in the late 1980s, little did he know that the language would become more famous than the popular programming languages such as C, C++, and Java. In fact, in the last couple of years, the programming environment witnessed a rapid growth in the number of languages available. If you've ever used older languages that were common in the 1960s and 1970s such as C, FORTRAN or COBOL, then you should know how much the programming environment has changed.

In recent years, object-oriented programming languages such as C++, JavaScript, Java, Golang and Python language have emerged as alternatives to core programming languages. Despite the large number of developments and the evolution that has occurred in programming, there is one language that cannot be overemphasized: Python.

Python language is beginner-friendly, yet very powerful. It is no wonder that today, the Python language is finding its applications in some of the most popular organizations such as Google, Pinterest, Mozilla, SurveyMonkey, SlideShare, YouTube, and Reddit as a core developer language. Today, Python is also being used to develop games and GUIs, perform data analysis, as well as to further advance the areas of machine learning and Artificial Intelligence.

What this means is that there are numerous career options that demand the use of Python language. Thus, learning Python can be the greatest asset for you to land that dream job! You can also boost your career with newly acquired Python programming skills.

In addition, Python's syntax is extremely simple to understand and follow regardless of whether you're a beginner or an advanced programmer. If you're an advanced programmer of C, C++, Java or Perl, you'll be sure to find the advanced part of programming in Python to be simple and will no doubt be able to accomplish great things with Python.

If you've already covered the basics in our latest series of programming books: "Python Programming: Comprehensive Guide for Beginners", you'll definitely find this book very interesting, especially in tackling complex problems more quickly than many other complex languages that have steeper learning curves.

Whom this book is written for

If you happen to have stumbled upon this book, then I'm assuming that you're interested in learning Python. This book is written for programmers who know the basics of the Python language but aren't experts. So, if you're a novice programmer, don't worry. Our latest book: "Python Programming: Comprehensive Guide for Beginners" has all the information that you need to begin programming in Python.

Once you've mastered all the beginner's concepts in Python programming, you can then try this: "Python Programming: Comprehensive Guide for Advanced Programmers". This book assumes that you've already mastered the basics of the syntax and have some fundamental experience in Python programming.

Ultimately, the book has been written for busy programmers that may want to find quick hacks that can automate complex and time-consuming tasks that are difficult to code in other languages.

What you expect to learn in this book

Here's what you can expect to learn in this book:

- Getting started with Python programming. This book will introduce you to the Python programming development environment.
- Iterators in Python. You'll begin to use Python iterators to help you manage complex decision structures in a simplified manner.
- Regular expressions in Python. Python's regular expressions will help you to express complex problems in a much simpler manner.
- Generators in Python
- Decorators in Python
- Context Managers in Python
- Descriptors in Python
- Metaprogramming with Python
- Python Scripting Blender
- Python Data Analysis Libraries. You'll be exposed to popular data analysis libraries such as NumPy and Panda.
- File Handling in Python. All the details of file handling such as opening an existing file, writing to an external file and merging of files will be covered.
- Refactoring Python code. You'll learn all the aspects of refactoring Python code and the tools for refactoring the Python code.

Applications of Python language

As I had mentioned earlier, Python language is the language being used to power applications in the following organizations: Google, Reddit, Mozilla, Pinterest, Yahoo, Facebook, CERN, and

NASA. As an experienced Python programmer, you will be able to accomplish many complex tasks that would have been difficult to complete in other programming languages.

If you're wondering the various areas in which Python language can be applied, simply take a look at your surroundings. From statistical data analysis to machine language, the list is simply endless. Here are some of the areas where Python language can be applied:

#1: Statistical Data Analysis

Python is a very powerful, open source and flexible language that data scientists can easily learn to perform data manipulation, management, and analysis. Its simple syntax—that resembles MatLab, C, or C++ is easy for any data scientist who is keen to learn it. Besides, Python combines the features of other general-purpose programming language and those of analytical and quantitative computing to bring out a robust language that can handle any data analysis in finance, research, oil or Signal Processing industries.

#2: Big Data and Data Analysis

These days, data scientists are overwhelmed by the problem of management of large volumes of data being churned out by organizations. One problem with the current method of data management is that it is unstructured, unlike the SQL data that current RDBMSs handle. Due to the challenge of the exponential growth and the uncoordinated means of processing of these sets of data because they are either structured or semi-structured, there is an urgent need for a language that can help you manage them efficiently.

The Python language can help you manage large volumes of data in a simple and efficient manner. Python language is shipped with in-built libraries such as NumPy, Panda, SciPy and Matplotlib that help you organize, manipulate and analyze these data.

#3: Finance

These days, it's atypical to find software developers in the finance industry armed with just one programming language. Now more than ever, demand for "full-stack" programmers who have experience with multiple languages is gaining a foothold in most institutions, including the financial industries. If there's one language that's common in all these industries—then it's Python.

For instance, J.P. Morgan uses Python to power its Athena system. The Bank of America Merrill Lynch has also built its Quartz system using Python. Have you ever wondered what language the popular financial system—the Stock Trading software—is programmed in? Well, the answer is none other than Python. Due to its object-oriented and multipurpose nature, Python is used in financial industries to improve pricing, risk management and manage the trading platforms.

#4: Artificial Intelligence (AI)

As previously mentioned, Python has inbuilt libraries that can help you develop natural language processing systems and machine learning systems. Some of the popular libraries that you'll find in Python that are used for AI development include:

- Scikit-learn for machine learning
- Theano for machine learning
- Tensor for machine learning
- Scrapy for natural language processing
- NLTK for natural language processing
- The pattern for natural language processing.

Chapter 3

Advanced Python Programming

Python language can be installed on MacOS and Linux platforms. More information about the Python language and its various versions can be found at the following official Python URL: http://www.python.org.

Getting started with Python

Ultimately, the first thing to get you started with Python programming is installing it on your computer. If you're using Windows OS, the process is pretty simple. Simply go to http://www.python.org and look for the latest version of Python (Python 3.0 is currently the latest version of Python), then download and install on your computer.

However, for MacOS, the process is not as straightforward. The latest versions of Mac OS (Mac OS X) and the Sierra already have Python 2.7 already installed in them. Therefore, You don't need to install it manually. However, for you to use the latest version of Python, which in this case is Python 3.0, you will have to use the Homebrew to update it.

For Linux users, you are to launch your Terminal application and type the following command at the command prompt: "su yum install python" if you're using a Debian Linux distribution such as Ubuntu. On the other hand, if you're using Red Hat/ RHEL/ CentOS Linux distributions such as Fedora, then type: "yum install python" at the command prompt and hit the enter key.

Once you've installed Python on your computer, you should identify the appropriate Text Editor to help you set the programming environment. The text editors will help you run the python programs from the command shell. As we'll be writing complex Python programs, I suggest that you identify an appropriate IDE that can automate some of the tasks so that you will be able to save time.

Personally, I recommend the Python IDLE. I have been using it for quite some time without encountering any problems. However, you are free to choose an IDE that suits you. For more information on getting started with Python including how to install Python on different platforms, the text editors to use, the structure of Python programs, the syntax rules and all the basics of Python language, get hold of our latest book: "Python Programming: Comprehensive Guide for Beginners".

In the latest book about Python programming for beginners, ensure that you master the following concepts:

- Structure of Python programs
- Variables and data types
- Python operators and how to use them in Python
- List data structure and its application
- Decision structures (if...else statements, the while loop, and switch statements).
- Python functions and modules
- Python classes
- Error handling and exceptions
- Program testing in Python

Chapter 4

Python Iterators

Before we begin using iterators, let's first define what Python iterators are.

Python iterators are simply objects that are used to support two methods that follow the iterator protocol. I know this can be quite difficult to understand at this stage, so let me break it down for you.

Suppose you open a file open a file and assign its results to a variable myiterator as follows:

```
myiterator = open('x')
```

In the above code, we have assigned a variable myiterator some results from a file. Now, suppose you want to print out the length of the lines in the file, here's what you'll do using the for ... loop:

```
for l in myiterator.readlines():
print len(l)
```

However, the same output can also be obtained using the code below:

```
for l in myiterator:
print len(l)
```

Which approach is simpler?

By looking at the two codes with a keen eye, you'll realize that the second approach is much simpler compared to the first one. Here's why:

- It is simpler and more elegant to represent the code using the second approach as compared to the first approach.
- The line of the file will not be read until it is required.

The first point is much clearer if you're used to functional programming. For instance, in functional programming, the statement:

```
print map(len,myiterator.readlines())
```

is not as simple and elegant as this statement:

```
print map(len,myiterator)
```

Similarly, the second point makes sense if the file was really large. The first method in the code above would require the entire file in memory. This is extremely undesirable considering the fact that you're supposed to come up with efficient programs that use little computer resources. With the second approach, you'll read just one line of the file at any given time. Obviously, you could also achieve the same functionality by calling the `readline()` instead of the `readlines()` which will not be as simple and elegant as the second approach.

So, what are we implying here?

In the second code, myiterator is acting as an iterator. Let me explain further.

Python language sequence is much like an array in other programming languages that you've learned and used. The array can take either one of the two forms, namely the list or tuples data structures. These sequence operations are much more flexible to use than when you're using a language such as C or C++. This is one of the reasons as to why Python is more powerful as compared to other languages.

In particular, you can have any function return a sequence, slice the sequences or even concatenate the sequence. Look at it this way, the iterator works like the sequence when you're using it but with the following major differences:

- You must write the function that constructs the sequence-like object
- The element of the "sequence" cannot be produced until you need it
- Unlike the real sequences, the iterator "sequence" can be infinitely long.

The python iterator objects are to support two methods while following the iterator rules. Here are the rules that iterators must follow:

__iter__ returns iterator object. This is only used in for ... and in ... statements.

__next__ method returns the next value from the iterator. If there are no more items to be returned, the StopIteration exception is raised, indicating that no more items can be returned.

Are you eager to see iterators in action?

Examine the Python code below:

```
class mycounter(object):
    def __init__(self, low, high):
        self.current = low
        self.high = high
    def __iter__(self):
        'This   section   returns   itself   as   an
iterator object'
        return self
    def __next__(self):
        'It returns the next value till current is
lower than the high value'
        if self.current >= self.high:
            raise StopIteration
        else:
            self.current += 1
            return self.current - 1
```

Once you've defined your class, it is now time to implement it using iterators. First, you have to instantiate your class. Open your Python console and type the following code:

```
olsen = mycounter(5,10)
for i in olsen:
...    print(i, end=' ')
```

Can you guess the output of the above code?

Well, if you're thinking of the following code, then you're correct.

```
5 6 7 8 9 10
```

Can you now explain why the iterator is printing this output?

Do note that the iterator object that you define in your code can be used only once. Once it has raised the StopIteration, it will continue raising the same exception. Here's the traceback that explains the sequence of operations:

```
>>> olsen = mycounter(5,6)
>>> next(olsen)
5
>>> next(olsen)
6
>>> next(olsen)
Traceback (most recent call the last):
File "<stdin>", line 1, in <module>
File "<stdin>", line 11, in next
StopIteration
>>> next(olsen)
Traceback (most recent call last):
File "<stdin>", line 1, in <module>
File "<stdin>", line 11, in next
StopIteration
```

Chapter 4 - Fun Challenges

Challenge 1

The main objective of this Challenge is to expose you to various concepts that you have learned about Python iterators such as how to create them and use them in your code.

What is the output of the following code?

```
class myclass(object):
    def __init__(self, low, high):
        self.current = low
        self.high = high
    def __iter__(self):
            return self
    def __next__(self):
        if self.current >= self.high:
            raise StopIteration
        else:
            self.current = self.current +10
            return self.current - 10
myindex = myclass(50,100)
for i in myindex:
print(i, end=' ')
```

Challenge 2

Use traceback to trace the output of the following Python code:

```
class myclass(object):
    def __init__(self, low, high):
        self.current = low
        self.high = high
    def __iter__(self):
            return self
    def __next__(self):
        if self.current >= self.high:
            raise StopIteration
        else:
            self.current = self.current +10
            return self.current - 10
myindex = myclass(50,100)
for i in myindex:
print(i, end=' ')
```

Chapter 4 - Solutions

Solution for Challenge 1

50,60,70,80,90,100

Solution for Challenge 2

```
>>> myindex = mycounter(50,60)
>>> next(myindex)
50
>>> next(myindex)
60
>>> next(myindex)
Traceback (most recent call the last):
File "<stdin>", line 1, in <module>
File "<stdin>", line 11, in next
StopIteration
>>> next(myindex)
Traceback (most recent call last):
File "<stdin>", line 1, in <module>
File "<stdin>", line 11, in next
StopIteration
```

Chapter 5

Python Generators

In the previous chapter, we have seen how iterators can help Python programmers in expressing their codes in a simpler and more elegant manner which makes programs more efficient. However, the key question is: How can we create the iterators in Python programming?

Well, Generators can help you to create the iterators. That's why they are called "Generators".

In terms of where Python programs should take us, generators can be viewed as functions that we can call repeatedly to create the iterators. However, unlike the ordinary functions, successive calls to the generator function will not start executing at the beginning of the function. Instead, the generator function will always resume the execution at the spot that was last exited.

In other words, the generator function always "picks up from where it left" as opposed to ordinary functions that always start afresh whenever they are called. Let me elaborate further with the use of an illustration for you to make more sense of what I just said.

You call the generator function just once. That call returns an iterator. In other words, it creates the iterator with `iter()` and the `next()` methods that can be invoked. The `next()` is similar to another function which implements using the idea of "picking-up-from-where-we-left". You can now either call the `next()` directly or use the iterator in the loop. The difference simply lies in the approach that you would like to take to implement your iterators and generators.

Whichever approach you take, do keep in mind that there are fundamental differences. Here are two major differences between the two approaches:

- When you use the iterators, the class can only be recognized by the Python interpreter as an iterator in the presence of the `iter()` and `next()` methods.

- When you use the generator, you don't have to set up the class. You simply write the plain function which will be easily be distinguished by the Python interpreter. However, you must use the `yield` instead of `return`, which is used in ordinary functions.

You should also note that the working mechanisms of `yield` and `return` are completely different from each other. When the yield statement is executed, the Python interpreter will record the line number of that statement (note that there can be several yield lines within the same generator). The next time the generator function is called with the same iterator, the function simply resumes the execution at the line following the `yield` statement.

Here is a summary of the main points on the `yield` statement when used with generators:

- The yield statement causes an exit from the function. However, the next time the function is called again; it starts off from where it left off. In other words, rather than at the start of the line, the function will be executed at the line following the yield statement.
- All the values of the local variables that existed at the time of the yield statement action will remain intact when the program resumes.
- There can be several yield lines within the same generator.

- You can use the return statements. However, its execution will result in the StopIteration exception being raised when the `next()` method is called again.
- The yield statement has one operand—or none—which is the return value. Such an operand can be a tuple.

After mastering the concepts of Generators, let us now look at an illustration.

The below example illustrates one of the most commonly used concepts in computer science: the Fibonacci series.

For a simple illustration, let's take a look at the good ol' Fibonacci numbers:

```
# fibgi,py, generator example; Fibonacci numbers
# fng = f_{n-1} + f_{n-2}
def fibonaci():
5 function2 = 1 # "f_{n-2}"
6 function1 = 1 # "f_{n-1}"
7 while True:
(function1,function2,oldfunction2)          =
(function1+function2,function1,function2)
yield oldfunction2

from fibg import *
g = fibonaci()
g.next()
1
g.next()
1
g.next()
2
g.next()
3
g.next()
5
g.next()
```

170

8

From the implementation of the Fibonacci series as seen above, you can see that we should resume the execution of the function in the middle of the code rather than at the top of the code. Therefore, we don't want to execute the code:

```
function2 = 1
```

In particular, the main point here is that the local variables `function1` and `function2` will retain their values between the calls. This is what will allow you to get away with using just the function instead of the class. This approach is much simpler and cleaner than the class-based approach. For example, in the code here we refer to `function1` instead of the `self.function1` as we usually do with the class-based versions.

When you're dealing with a complex function, simplifications using the generators can add readability to your Python code. This property of retaining the local variables between calls is akin to declaring static local variables, something that you're already familiar with. However, do note that in Python language you can set several instances of the generator function with each instance maintaining different values for local variables.

If you wish to achieve the same functionality in a language like C, you will have to use arrays with local variables that are indexed by instance numbers. In fact, to implement the generator in C, you are still required to use the tedious method of employing the use of C's ordinary return statement that labels the statements following the various return lines.

Chapter 5 – Fun Challenges

These Challenges test you on practical applications of Python generators.

Challenge 3

Assume you are writing a file browser that displays files line by line. The list of files is being defined on the commands line (in sys.argv). Now, after displaying one line, the program waits for a user input where the user can perform the following actions:

- Hit the Enter to display the next line
- Hit the n + Enter to forget the rest of the current file and begin with the next file
- Hit any Key + Enter to display the next line

The first part of the code has already been written: it is simply a function that displays the lines and queries the user enters for input. Now your job is to write the second part which is a generator that read_lines with the following interface: during construction, it is passed a list of files to be read. If yields the line after line from the first file, then from the second file, and so on.

When the last file has been exhausted, it stops. The user of the generator can also throw any exception into the generator using (SkipThisFile) signal which informs the generator to skip the rest of the current file, and just produce a dummy value that should be skipped. Here is the interface of Python environment. Your task is to write the other code according to the instructions above.

```
class SkipThisFile(Exception):
pass
def read_lines(*files):
#
for file in files:
yield 'dummy line'
def display_files(*files):
source = read_lines(*files)
for line in source:
print(line, end='')
myinp = input()
if myinp == 'n':
print('NEXT')
source.throw(SkipThisFile)    #    return    value    is
ignored
```

Challenge 4

Write a generator that returns a few values. Launch it and retrieve any value using next which is the global function. Throw any exception that arises.

Chapter 5 - Solutions

Solution for Challenge 3

```
def read_mylines(*files):
for file in files:
for myline in open(file):
try:
yield line.rstrip('\n')
except SkipThisFile:
yield 'dummy'
break
```

Solution for Challenge 4

```
def logged(myfunc):
def wrapper(*args, **kwargs):
print('Return                          values'
{.__name__}({}{}{})'.format(val    =    func(*args,
**kwargs)
print('it returned', val)
return val
return wrapper
```

Chapter 6

Regular Expressions

Regular expressions are a special sequence of characters that can help to match or find other strings using a specialized syntax that is contained in a pattern. In Python language, the regular expressions can help you to match strings, concatenate strings, merge and even unmerge strings using patterns. The module `re` in Python gives full support for Perl-like regular expressions in Python language.

On the other hand, the module `re.error` is used to handle exceptions and errors that arise when one is using regular expressions in Python language. In this chapter, we will explore all programming aspects of regular expressions in Python. First things first, even before you begin learning how to use regular expressions, it is important that you understand the various functions that have special meanings when used in regular expressions. Knowing these functions will help you avoid to confusion when dealing with regular expressions in Python.

Regular Expression Functions

Below are the some of the most commonly used functions in Python's regular expressions:

#1: Match Function

This function tries to match the regular expression pattern to the string with optional flags.

Below is the syntax for the match function:

```
re.match(pattern, string, flags=0)
```

- The pattern in the function above is the regular expression that you want to match.
- The string is the string that would be searched to match the pattern at the start of the string.
- You can specify the different flags using the bitwise OR operator (|) as a modifier. There are two modifiers namely the `group(num=0)` and `groups()`. The modifier `group(num=0)` returns the entire match for the regular expression. On the other hand, the modifier `groups()` returns all the matching subgroups in the tuple.

Below is an example of how you can use the match function for regular expressions in a Python code:

```
import re
msentence=  "Do   you   think   cats   are   smarter   than
dogs?"
matchingObj  =  re.match(  r'(.*)  are  (.*?)  .*',
msentence,  re.M|re.I)
if matchingObj:
print        "matchingObj.group()            :          ",
matchingObj.group()
print          "matchingObj.group(1)         :          ",
matchingObj.group(1)
print          "matchingObj.group(2)         :          ",
matchingObj.group(2)
else:
print "There is no match!"
```

What do you think the above code will produce when executed?

Well, here's the output of the code:

```
matchingObj.group()  :  Do  you  think  that  cats  are
smarter than dogs
matchingObj.group(1)  :  Do
matchingObj.group(2)  :  think
```

#2: Search function

As the name suggests, the search function searches for the first occurrence of regular expression pattern within a string with the optional flags.

The search function has the following syntax:

```
re.search(pattern, string, flags=0)
```

- The pattern in the function above is the regular expression that you want to search.
- The string is the string that would be searched to match the pattern at the start of the string.
- You can specify the different flags using the bitwise OR operator (|) as a modifier. There are two modifiers namely the `group(num=0)` and `groups()`. The modifier `group(num=0)` returns the entire match for the regular expression. On the other hand, the modifier `groups()` returns all the matching subgroups in the tuple.

Below is an example of how you can use the search function in regular expressions:

```
import re
msentence = "Do you think cats are smarter than
dogs?";
searchingObj = re.search( r'(.*) are (.*?) .*',
msentence, re.M|re.I)
if searchingObj:
print        "searchingObj.group()        :        ",
searchingObj.group()
print        "searchingObj.group(1)        :        ",
searchingObj.group(1)
print        "searchingObj.group(2)        :        ",
searchingObj.group(2)
else:
print "Nothing has been found!!"
```

The above code will produce the following results when executed:

```
matchingObj.group():  Do  you  think  that  cats  are
smarter than dogs
matchingObj.group(1)  :  Do
matchingObj.group(2)  :  think
```

#3: Search and Replace

The search and replace method is implemented using the **sub** method. Below is a syntax:

```
re.sub(pattern, repl, string, max=0)
```

The sub method is used to replace all the occurrences of the regular expression pattern in the string with the `repl` string, substituting all occurrences unless the `max` is provided. This method returns the modified string.

Here's an example:

```
import re
myphoneno = "+254-722-848386 # This is my phone
number"
mynum = re.sub(r'#.*$', "", myphoneno)
print "My Phone Num is : ", mynum
# Remove anything other than digits
mynum = re.sub(r'\D', "", myphoneno)
print "My Phone Num is: ", mynum
```

When executed the above code will produce the following output:

```
My Phone Num is: +254-722-848386
My Phone Num is: 254722848386
```

Regular Express Modifiers

The regular expression literals that you can have an optional modifier that controls various aspects of the matching process. The modifiers are specified as an optional flag. Multiple modifiers can be specified using the exclusive OR (|) operator.

Below are common examples of these modifiers and their descriptions:

- `re.I`. It is used to performs case-insensitive matching in the regular expression.
- `Re.L`. It is used to interpret the words according to their current location. This interpretation can affect the alphabetic group (\w and \W) and the word boundary behavior (\b and \B).
- `re.M`. It is used to make the $ match the end of the line (not just the completion of the string) and makes the ^ match the beginning of any line (not just the beginning of the string).
- `re.S`. It specifies a period (dot) match for any character, including the newline.
- `re.U`. It interprets the letters according to the Unicode character set. It affects the behavior of \w, \W, \b, \B characters.
- `re.X`. It allows the "cuter" regular expression syntax. It ignores the whitespace (except when used inside the set [] or when escaped by the backslash).

Regular Expression Patterns

So far, we've examined the modifiers and functions. What about regular expression patterns?

Well, the regular expression patterns are the indicators that help the interpreter to determine how the characters should be matched or searched. Now, except for the control characters (+? * ^ $ ( ) [ ] { } | \) all the other characters can match themselves. If you want to escape the control character, you can do so by preceding it with a backslash character.

Below are common regular expression patterns:

```
^ It matches the beginning of the line.
$ It matches the end of the line.
. It matches any single character except the
newline. When you use the m option, it allows it
to match the newline as well.
[...]. It matches any single character within the
brackets.
[^...]. It matches any single character that is
not in brackets
re* It matches 0 or more occurrences of the
preceding expression.
re+ It matches 1 or more occurrence of the
preceding expression.
re? It matches 0 or 1 occurrences of the preceding
expression.
re{ n}. It matches exactly n number of occurrences
of the preceding expression.
re{ n,}. It matches n or more occurrences of the
preceding expression.
re{ n, m}. It matches at least n and at most m
occurrences of the preceding expression.
a| b. It matches either a or b in the regular
expression.
(re) It groups the regular expressions and
remembers the matched text.
(? imx). It temporarily toggles on the i, m, or x
options within the regular expression. If it is in
the parentheses, only the area is affected.
(?-imx). It temporarily toggles off the i, m, or x
options within the regular expression. If in
parentheses, only the area will be affected.
(?: re) Groups regular expressions without
remembering matched text.
(?imx: re). It temporarily toggles on the i, m, or
x options within the parentheses.
```

(?-imx: re). It temporarily toggles off the i, m, or x options within the parentheses.

(?#...) This is a comment

(?= re) Indicates the position using the pattern. It doesn't have a specific range.

(?! re) Indicates the position using the pattern negation. It does not have a range.

(?> re) It matches the independent pattern without backtracking.

\w It matches the word characters.

\W It matches the non-word characters.

\s It matches the whitespace which is equivalent to [\t\n\r\f].

\S It matches the non-whitespace.

\d It matches the digits which is equivalent to [0-9].

\D It matches the non-digits.

\A It matches start of a string.

\Z It matches the end of string. If a newline exists, it will match just before the newline.

\z It matches the end of string.

\G It matches the point where last match finished.

\b It matches the word boundaries when outside brackets.

Chapter 6 – Fun Challenges

The objectives of these Challenges are to assess your understanding of Python's ability to handle patterns, modifiers, and strings in regular expressions.

Challenge 5

Write a Python program that finds all the adverbs and their positions in a given sentence. For instance, the program should find all the adverbs and their positions in a sentence such as "Well, the regular expression patterns are the indicators that help the interpreter to determine how the characters should be matched or searched. Now, except for the control characters (+? * ^ $ ( ) [ ] { } | \) all the other characters can match themselves. If you want to escape the control character, you can do it by preceding it with a backslash character."

Challenge 6

Write a Python program that removes words from a string of length between 1 and any given number. Consider the following text as your input: "Well, the regular expression patterns are the indicators that help the interpreter to determine how the characters should be matched or searched. Now, except for the control characters (+? * ^ $ ( ) [ ] { } | \) all the other characters can match themselves. If you want to escape the control character, you can do it by preceding it with a backslash character."

Chapter 6 - Solutions

Solution for Challenge 5

```
import re
mytext = " Well, the regular expression patterns
are the indicators that help the interpreter to
determine how the characters should be matched or
searched. Now, except for the control characters
(+? * ^ $ ( ) [ ] { } | \) all the other
characters can match themselves. If you want to
escape the control character, you can do it by
preceding it with a backslash character."
for m in re.finditer(r"\w+ly", mytext):
    print('%d-%d:    %s'  %  (m.start(),   m.end(),
m.group(0)))
```

Solution for Challenge 6

```
import re
mytext = "Well, the regular expression patterns
are the indicators that help the interpreter to
determine how the characters should be matched or
searched. Now, except for the control characters
(+? * ^ $ ( ) [ ] { } | \) all the other
characters can match themselves. If you want to
escape the control character, you can do it by
preceding it with a backslash character."
shortword = re.compile(r'\W*\b\w{1,50}\b')
print(shortword.sub('', text))
```

Chapter 7

Python Decorators

Python decorators provide a simple syntax and an efficient way of calling higher-order functions. At the outset, a Python decorator is just like the ordinary function that you're already familiar with. However, the decorator usually takes in another function and extends its behavior to the latter function without modifying it explicitly.

The reason why decorators have been included in Python is to improve the language's flexibility. Python is ported with a rich set of powerful features and expressive syntax. One of the ways of expressing the syntax differently is through the Python decorators. In the context of design patterns, the decorators alter the functionality of any function, method or class that you've specified in your code dynamically without directly using the subclasses.

Why is this important?

Well, using decorators is ideal anytime you want to extend the functionality of your functions; it is much easier in your code. In fact, you can implement the decorator pattern anywhere in your Python code. The Python decorators work as program wrappers, modifying the behavior of your code before and after a target function has been executed. This is done automatically without your involvement. In this case, decorators will be working as "cleaners" of your code.

Characteristics of Python function

Before we dive deeper into decorators, here are a couple of things that you should know about functions:

1. **Functions can be defined inside other functions**. The code below illustrates how you can define a function inside another function:

```
def greetings(myname):
    def get_message():
        return "Hello Tim!"
    result = get_message()+myname
    return result
print greetings("Tim!")
```

When executed, the above code outputs the following:

```
Hello Tim!
```

2. *Functions can also be passed as parameters to other functions*. The code below illustrates how you can pass functions as parameters to other functions:

```
def greetings(myname):
return "Hello " + name
def call_func(func):
    other_name = "Hello Tim!"
 return func(other_name)
print call_func(greetings)
```

When executed, the above code outputs the following:

```
Hello Tim!
```

3. *Functions can also return other functions in Python.* In other words, functions can generate other functions.

```
def compose_greet_func():
    def get_message():
        return "Hello Tim!"
    return get_message
greetings = compose_greet_func()
print greetings()
```

When executed, the above code outputs the following:

```
Hello Tim!
```

Now that you've refreshed your memory about functions, the process of wrapping functions to other existing functions can now make sense to you. In the example below, let's consider a basic function that wraps the string output of another function by the p tags.

```
def get_text(myname):
    return      "lorem      ipsum,      {0}      dolor      sit
amet".format(myname)

def p_decorate(func):
    def func_wrapper(myname):
        return "<p>{0}</p>".format(func(myname))
    return func_wrapper
my_get_text = p_decorate(get_text)
print my_get_text("Tim")
# <p>Outputs lorem ipsum, Tim dolor sit amet</p>
```

Do you know you've just created your first Python decorators?
In the above code, you've just created a function that can take
another function as an argument and then generate a new
function while augmenting the work of the original function.
The resulting function returns the generated function that can
be used anywhere in the code. For instance, to have the
get_text itself be decorated by the p_decorate, you are to
assign the get_text to the result of the p_decorate.

Decorators Syntax

That is how the decorators can be created. Generally, Python
decorators have the following syntax:

```
@deco
def myfunc():
print 'in myfunc
```

The above code is similar to:

```
def myfunc():
print 'in myfunc'
myfunc = deco(myfunc)
```

Python makes the process of creating and using decorators simpler and more efficient for a programmer. For instance, to decorate the `get_text` in our earlier example, you don't have to use the `get_text = p_decorator(get_text)`. Instead, you can simply name the decorator that is appended with the @ symbol.

Our earlier example will now appear as follows if the syntax of decorators is used:

```
def p_decorate(myfunc):
    def myfunc_wrapper(name):
        return "<p>{0}</p>".format(myfunc(myname))
    return func_wrapper

@p_decorate
def get_text(myname):
    return     "lorem     ipsum,     {0}     dolor     sit
amet".format(name)

print get_text("Tim")
```

The above code will output the following:

```
<p>lorem ipsum, Tim dolor sit amet</p>
```

Decorating Methods

In Python language, the methods are functions that expect their first argument to be a reference of some current object. You can build decorators for the methods in the same way while taking care of the wrapper function.

Consider the code below:

```
def p_decorate(myfunc):
    def func_wrapper(myself):
        return "<p>{0}</p>".format(func(myself))
    return func_wrapper
class Person(myobject):
    def __init__(self):
        self.name = "Peter"
        self.family = "Williams"
    @p_decorate
    def get_fullname(myself):
        return self.name+" "+myself.family
my_person = Person()
print my_person.get_fullname()
```

Even though the above code has been used to decorate the methods, a much better approach would have been to make the decorator useful for the functions and methods alike. This can be achieved by placing *args and **kwargs as the parameters for the wrapper.

The wrapper can then accept an arbitrary number of arguments and keyword arguments. Here's how the code should look like:

```
def p_decorate(myfunc):
    def func_wrapper(*args, **kwargs):
        return     "<p>{0}</p>".format(myfunc(*args,
**kwargs))
    return func_wrapper
class Person(myobject):
    def __init__(myself):
        self.name = "Peter"
        self.family = "Williams"
    @p_decorate
    def get_fullname(myself):
        return self.name+" "+myself.family
my_person = Person()
print my_person.get_fullname()
```

Chapter 7 - Challenges

These Challenges tests you on the concepts of defining decorators as wrapper functions and classes.

Challenge 7

Define a decorator which wraps functions to the log function arguments and the returns value on each call. Your wrapper function should define both the *args and the **kwargs and print them both as follows:

```
>>> @logged
... def myfunc(*args):
... return 3 + len(args)
>>> myfunc(4, 4, 4)
you called myfunc(4, 4, 4)
it returned 6
6
```

Challenge 8

Write a decorator that caches the function invocation results. Store the pairs arg: result in a dictionary in an attribute of the function object that you have defined. The function being conceptualized is:

```
def myfibonacci(n):
assert n >= 0
if n < 2:
return n
else:
return myfibonacci(n-1) + myfibonacci(n-2)
```

Chapter 7 - Solutions

Solution for Challenge 7

```
def logged(myfunc):
#Print out the arguments before function call and
after the call print out the returned value #
def wrapper(*args, **kwargs):
print('You                              called
{.__name__}({}{}{})'.format(myfunc,
str(list(args))[1:-1],       # Cast this to the list
is because tuple of length one has an extra comma#
', ' if kwargs else '',
', '.join('{}={}'.format(*pair)   for   pair   in
kwargs.items()),
))
val = myfunc(*args, **kwargs)
print('It returned', val)
return val
return wrapper
```

Solution for Challenge 8

```
def memoize(func):
func.cache = {}
def wrapper(n):
try:
ans = func.cache[n]
except KeyError:
ans = func.cache[n] = func(n)
return ans
return wrapper
@conceptualize
def myfibonacci(n):
"""
>>> print(myfibonacci.cache)
{}
>>> myfibonacci(1)
1
>>> myfibonacci(2)
1
>>> myfibonacci(10)
55
>>> myfibonacci.cache[10]
55
>>> myfibonacci(40)
102334155
"""
assert n >= 0
if n < 2:
return n
else:
return myfibonacci(n-1) + myfibonacci(n-2)
```

Chapter 8

Python Descriptors

This chapter explores Python descriptors, their syntax, how they are called and several built-in Python descriptors, including the functions, the properties, and the static methods. Let's jump right in.

What are Python descriptors?

Python descriptors are simply objects that you can create. However, these objects must have an attribute with the "binding behavior". I know you're now thinking, "What the hell is this binding behavior?"

Well, the descriptors that you create must have attributes which can be overridden by methods such as the __get__(), the `__set__()`, and the `__delete__()` in the descriptor protocol. If any of these methods have been defined for an object, then that object is said to be a descriptor. Learning how to use Python descriptors not only gives you access to a larger programming toolset, but also creates a deeper understanding of how the language works.

The default behavior for all the attribute access is the get, the set, or the delete methods. For instance, `myname.x` has a lookup that starts with the `myname.__dict__['x']`, and then moves to `type(myname).__dict__['x']`, and continues all the way to base classes of the `type(myname)`, excluding the metaclasses.

The descriptors are powerful general-purpose protocols that you can utilize to implement new style classes. Descriptors are the mechanisms behind the properties, the methods, the static methods and class methods that are used in Python language to simplify the language and make it more flexible.

Descriptor Protocols

There are three basic protocols that are used for descriptors:

- `descr.__get__(self, obj, type=None)` for valued descriptors
- `descr.__set__(self, obj, value)` for none descriptors

- `descr.__delete__(self, obj)` for none descriptors.

When you define any of the above methods, the object is then considered to be a descriptor and can override the default behavior upon being looked up as an attribute. If the descriptor defines both the `__get__()` and the `__set__()` methods, it is considered a data descriptor. On the other hand, descriptors that only define the `__get__()` are called non-data descriptors.

The data and non-data descriptors differ in how the overriding is computed with regards to the entries in the dictionary. If an instance's dictionary has an entry containing the name as a data descriptor, then the data descriptor will take precedence. On the other hand, if an instance's dictionary has an entry that contains the same name as the non-data descriptor, then the dictionary entry will take the precedence.

How to invoke the descriptors

Descriptors can be called directly by using their method names such as `myname.__get__(obj)`. Alternatively, a descriptor can be invoked automatically upon the attribute access. For instance, `obj.d` will look up for d in the dictionary for obj. Now, suppose d defines the method `__get__()`, then `d.__get__(obj)` is automatically invoked.

Here is a summary of what you should know about invoking the descriptors:

- The descriptors are usually invoked by the __getattribute__() method.
- The overriding __getattribute__() method prevents automatic descriptor calls.
- The __getattribute__() is only available with the new style classes and objects.
- The object __getattribute__() and the type.__getattribute__() will make different calls to the __get__().
- The data descriptors will always override the instance dictionaries.
- The non-data descriptors can be overridden by the instance dictionaries.

Let us now look at a practical example of descriptors in action!

The Python code below creates a class whose objects are data descriptors. These descriptors print a message for each of the get or set methods. The overriding __getattribute__() is an alternate approach that can be done for every attribute.

```
class RevealAccess(object):
    #This data descriptor sets and returns values
normally and prints a message logging their
access.#
    def        __init__(myself,        initval=None,
name='var'):
        self.val = initval
        self.name = name
    def __get__(myself, obj, objtype):
        print 'Retrieving', myself.name
```

```
            return myself.val
      def __set__(myself, obj, val):
            print 'Updating', myself.name
            self.val = val
>>> class MyClass(object):
...       mydesc = RevealAccess(10, 'var "mydesc"')
...       y = 5
>>> m = MyClass()
>>> m.desc
Retrieving var "mydesc"
10
>>> m.desc = 20
Updating var "mydesc"
>>> m.desc
Retrieving var "mydesc"
20
>>> m.y
5
```

Functions and Methods

The Python's object oriented features have been developed around the function-based environment. Using the non-data descriptors, the two have been merged seamlessly to produce a language that's not only simple and flexible to use, but is also powerful enough to represent enough inbuilt functions for programmers.

The class dictionaries are used to store the methods as functions. In any class definition, the methods are usually written using the def and lambda—the usual tools and syntax for creating functions. The only difference from the regular functions is that the first argument will always be reserved for the object instance. By convention, the instance reference is called self but it may also be called any other variable name that a programmer selects.

Now, to support the method calls, the functions must include the __get__() method that binds methods during the attribute access. This implies that all the functions are essentially non-data descriptors that return bound or unbound methods depending on whether they have been invoked from an object or a class. In pure Python, this is how you can achieve this feat:

```python
class Function(object):
    def __get__(self, obj, objtype=None):
        "Simulate    the    func_descr_get()    in
Objects/funcobject.c"
        return    types.MethodType(self,    obj,
objtype)
```

Running the Python interpreter will show how the function descriptor works in practice:

```python
>>>>>> class M(object):
...      def f(self, mydesc):
...          return mydesc
...
>>> d = M()
>>> M.__dict__['f']    # Store it internally as a
function
<function f at 0x00C45070>
>>> M.f                     # Get from a class which
becomes an unbound method
<unbound method M.f>
>>> M.f                     # Get it from an instance
which becomes a bound method
<bound   method   M.f   of   <__main__.D   object   at
0x00B18C90>>
```

The output indicates that both the bound and unbound methods are two different types. While they have been implemented this way, the actual C implementation of the `PyMethod_Type` in the "`Objects/classobject.c`"is a single object that has two different representations depending on whether the `im_self` field has been set or is NULL—which is the C equivalent of none.

Similarly, the effects of calling the method object will depend on the `im_self` field. If it is set—meaning it is bound—then the original function which is stored in the `im_func field`) will be called with the first parameter set to the instance. If it is unbound, then all of the arguments will be passed unchanged to the original function.

Static Methods and Class Methods

The non-data descriptors can provide a simple mechanism for the variations on the usual patterns of binding functions into the methods. To recap what we have learnt thus far, all the functions that have the `__get__()` method can be converted to a method where they are accessed as attributes. The non-data descriptor can transform the `obj.f(*args)` calls into `f(obj, *args)`. When the `klass.f(*args)` is called, it automatically becomes `f(*args)`.

The static methods return the underlying function without the changes. Calling either the `c.f` or the `C.f` is similar to the direct lookup into the `object.__getattribute__(c, "f")` or the `object.__getattribute__(C, "f")`. Consequently, the function automatically becomes identically accessible from either the object or the class.

Good programming practice demands that the static methods should not reference the `self`-variable. For example, a statistics package can have a container class for the experimental data. The class may provide normal methods for computing the mean, the median, and any other descriptive statistics that can be done on the data.

However, there can also be useful functions that are conceptually related but don't rely on the data that you would like to use. For instance, the `erf(x)` can come in handy during the conversion routine with your statistical data even though it does not directly depend on any dataset in particular. In this instance, it can be called either from the object or from the class as follows:

```
s.erf(1.5)  --> .9332
```

Or

```
sample.erf(1.5)  --> .9332.
```

This is because the static methods can return the underlying function with no changes.

Chapter 8 - Challenges

The main aim of these Challenges is to test you on how you can use the following Descriptor objects in Python:

- a) The __get__ method
- b) The __set__ method
- c) The __delete__ method

Challenge 9

What is the output of the following Python code?

```
class Descriptor(object):
    def __init__(self):
        self._name = ''
    def __get__(self, instance, owner):
        print "Getting the information: %s" %
self._name
        return self._name
    def __set__(self, instance, name):
        print "Setting the information: %s" % name
        self._name = name.title()
    def __delete__(self, instance):
        print "Deleting the information: %s"
%self._name
        del self.name
class Person(object):
    name = Descriptor()
```

Challenge 10

Rewrite the code below that has descriptors using the property type:

```
class Descriptor(object):
    def __init__(self):
        self._name = ''
    def __get__(self, instance, owner):
        print "Getting   the   information:   %s"   %
self._name
        return self._name
    def __set__(self, instance, name):
        print "Setting the information: %s" % name
        self._name = name.title()
    def __delete__(self, instance):
        print   "Deleting   the   information:   %s"
%self._name
        del self.name
class Person(object):
    name = Descriptor()
```

Chapter 8 - Solutions

Solution for Challenge 9

```
>>> user = Person()
>>> user.name = 'Peter James'
Setting the information: Peter James
>>> user.name
Getting the information: Peter James
'Peter James'
>>> del user.name
Deleting: Peter James
```

Solution for Challenge 10

```
class Person(object):
    def __init__(self):
        self._name = ''
    def fget(self):
        print "Getting the information: %s" %
self._name
        return self._name
    def fset(self, value):
        print "Setting the information: %s" %
value
        self._name = value.title()
    def fdel(self):
        print "Deleting the information: %s"
%self._name
        del self._name
    name = property(fget, fset, fdel, "I'm the
property.")
```

Chapter 9

Metaprogramming

Loosely defined, Metaprogramming refers to programs that can manipulate their own program structure, such as functions, classes, or the structure of other programs, such as data. To understand the concept of Metaprogramming, you will have to understand how classes and objects are defined in Python language.

Python objects are created by other objects which are special objects that we call classes. In this regard, classes can also be regarded as objects. However, classes are modified in a slightly different manner as compared to objects.

Consider the following code:

```
>>> class MyClass: pass
>>> MyClass.field = 1200
>>> someclass = MyClass()
>>> someclass.field
1200
>>> MyClass.field2 = 2000
>>> someclass.field2
5000
>>> MyClass.method = lambda self: "Hello!"
>>> someclass.method()
```

To modify such a class, all you need to do is to assume that you're dealing with an object. You can add and remove methods that you have defined. The only difference is that any change that you make to a particular class will affect all the objects of the class, even the ones that you've already instantiated.

Type metaclass

A fundamental question that we should ask is this: What makes these special "classes" objects?

Well, other special objects called metaclasses are the ones that are enabling you to work with classes as though you were dealing with objects. At the outset, the default metaclass—which is often referred to as the type class—is the one that is helping you to work with your classes the correct way. In some cases, however, you can leverage the type class by modifying the manner in which these classes are created.

Typically, you can achieve this by performing extra actions or injecting a new code. If this is the case, then you can use the metaclass programming to modify the manner in which your objects are being created. Ideally, the classes and objects that you're creating will help you to manipulate other program structures—such as the functions, classes—or even the structure of other programs such as data. This is what Metaprogramming in Python is.

It is worth noting that in the majority of Python programming cases, you may not need to use the metaclasses since using them in your code can be overwhelming. However, in cases, where you're dealing with objects and classes that are confusing, it is crucial for you to adopt the metaclass approach.

Some of the functionalities that were previously available with metaclasses are now available in a more simplified form when you use the class decorators. However, it is still important to understand how Metaprogramming can help you achieve certain results without using the decorators.

Essentials of Python Metaprogramming

Now that you know that metaclasses can create classes, and the classes can create instances, you can create any class or object that you want. That's the main idea of Metaprogramming. Conventionally, when you create a class, its default metaclass is automatically invoked to create that class that you've just defined. The funny thing is you don't know that this is happening since it takes place in the background!

To explicitly code the metaclass creation, all you have to do is to call the type class with one argument that will generate information on the existing class. When you call the type class with three arguments, it also creates a new class object. Therefore, the number of arguments that you use when calling the type object is crucial. As such, the arguments that you'll use when invoking type object are as follows:

- The name of the class
- The list of base classes
- The dictionary that gives the namespace for the class with all the fields and methods.

For instance, instead of:

```
class MyClass: pass
```

You can use this:

```
MyClass = type ('My Data', (), {})
```

You can also add the base classes, fields and methods as follows:

```
def mydata(self, you):
    print("How are, " + you)
MyList = type('MyList', (list,), dict(x=100, How
are you=How are you))
ml = MyList()
ml.append("Peter")
```

```
print(ml)
print(ml.x)
ml.mydata("Sam")
print(ml.__class__.__class__)
```

When executed, the above code produces the following output:

```
['Peter']
1000
How are you, Peter
```

Do note that printing of the class of the class will result in the metaclass. The ability to produce classes programmatically using the type opens up interesting possibilities for Python programmers.

The Metaclass Hook

So far, we've only focused on the metaclass type directly. The metaclass programming encompasses hooking your own operations into the creation of other class objects. This can be accomplished by:

- Writing a subclass of the metaclass type.
- Inserting that new metaclass into the class development process using a metaclass hook.

The metaclass hook will be a static field in the class called the __metaclass__. In an ordinary sense, this class will not be assigned so the Python will just create the class. However, if you define the __metaclass__ to the point that is callable, then Python will call the __metaclass__() after the initial creation of the class object and then pass it in the class object, class name, followed by the list of base classes and the accompanying namespace dictionary.

By convention, when specifying the metaclasses, `cls` is usually used rather than the self as the first argument to all the methods except the ___new___() with `cls` being the class object is being changed. The practice of calling the base-class constructor first using the `super()` in the derived-class constructor should always be followed by the metaclasses as well.

Here's an example:

```
class MyClass(object):
    class __metaclass__(type):
        def __init__(cls, name, bases, nmspc):
            type.__init__(cls, name, bases, nmspc)
            cls.uses_metaclass = lambda self :
"Hello!"
class MyClass2(MyClass2): pass
MyClass = MyClass2()
print simple.uses_metaclass()
```

The code above will print the following output:

```
Hello!
```

In the example as seen above, the compiler will not accept the `super()` call because it is indicating ___metaclass___ which hasn't been defined yet, forcing the interpreter to use the specific call to the `type.__init__()`.

Chapter 9 - Challenges

Challenge 11

```
What is the output of the following code?
def mydata(self, you):
    print("How are, " + you)
MyList = type('MyList', (list,), dict(x=5000, How
are you=How are you))
myl = MyList()
myl.append("Jennifer Lynn")
print(myl)
print(myl.x)
myl.mydata("Dennish Fred")
print(myl.__class__.__class__)
```

Challenge 12

What is the difference between a metaclass and a class in

Python?

Chapter 9 - Solutions

Solution for Challenge 11

```
['Jennifer Lynn']
5000
How are you, Jennifer Lynn
```

Solutions for Challenge 12

Metaclasses allow programmers to work with classes as though they are dealing with objects. However, classes don't allow programmers to work with other classes as though they are dealing with objects.

Chapter 10

Python Scripting Blender

This chapter explores one of Python's powerful features of incorporating 3D images and animations for the development of games. By the end of the chapter, you'll have a view of the big picture of all aspects of Python's 3D image creation and animations.

Let's start with the fundamental question: What is a Python Blender?

What is a Python Blender?

Well, a Python Blender is a powerful 3D application tool that has been included in Python as a library for creating 3D images and animations. Using the Python Blender, you can bring out your creativity when developing your programs. The main strength of the Python Blender is that it provides a smooth and seamless workflow for the programmers.

By interacting with several buttons and the menu using a keyboard and mouse, you can create objects, sculpt them and even rig these objects. Besides creating objects using devices, Python Blender also enables you to create objects and other applications using a scripting interface. The Python scripting interface provides extensive tools with almost all of the functionalities that you'll require when dealing with 3D images and animations.

How to access Python's Blender Built-in Python Console

Ultimately, the first step towards using the Python's Blender is accessing the inbuilt Python console. It is only by accessing the console will you be able to begin to program. By pressing the SHIFT+F4 in any Blender window such as 3D View, Timeline, you can change it to a console view and begin working with scripts.

For you to have an idea of what the Python Blender and scripting is like, you should first understand all the application modules available in Python Blender.

Application classes in the Blender

The Python Blender can be imported into any application using the below statement:

```
import bpy
```

In the above example, `bpy` is the Python Blender that you want to use in your code. However, the `bpy` module has several classes that will help you to create several objects. Below are some examples of these classes:

- `bpy.context`. It contains all the settings' information such as the current 3D mode, which objects have been selected, and so on.
- `bpy.data`.
  This is where you'll find the contents of the current docu ment, whether they are existing on the scene or not.
- `bpy.ops`. It contains operators that perform the actual functions of Blender. These operators can be attached to the hotkeys, buttons or even be called from a script. When you create an add-on script, it will automatically define new operators, where every operator must have a unique name.
- `bpy.types`. It has all the information about the different types of objects in the `bpy.data`.
- `bpy.utils`. It contains the Blender utilities
- `bpy.path`. It contains information about the path and is similar to `os.path`
- `bpy.app`. It contains information about the application's data.
- `bpy.props`. It contains functions for defining the properties that allow your scripts to attach custom information to a scene.

Now that you've examined the Python Blender, its modules, and classes, let's dive in and find out what you can do with this powerful library.

How to manipulate selection on a 3D surface

The following code illustrates how you can manipulate the selection on any 3D surface by using Python Blender:

```
bpy.ops.transform.rotate(value = 65, axis = (2, 1,
 1))  # Operations that  apply only to the selection
that          you         have          selected.
bpy.ops.transform.translate(value = (1, 1, 2))
bpy.ops.transform.resize(value = (1, 1, 0))
bpy.ops.object.material_slot_add()
bpy.ops.object.rotation_clear()
bpy.data.objects['Cube'].location += mathutils.Vec
tor((1, 1, 1))
```

The first line of the code shows how you can transform (rotate) an object by an angle of 65 at the coordinators (2, 1, 1). Please note that before you begin using the Python Blender, you must first import it into your code using the statement below:

```
import bpy
```

The second, third, fourth and fifth lines show how you can apply specific transformations to any surface of your 3D device.

Manipulating the vertex coordinates

You can manipulate the vertex coordinates on a 3D surface by using the following code:

```
import bpy #Importing the Blender in the code
```

```
for item in bpy.data.objects:
print(item.name) #Printing the items
if item.type == 'MESH':#Manipulating    the    local
coordinates
for vertex in item.data.vertices: print(vertex.co)
```

Let's examine another example that applies to world

coordinates:

```
import bpy #Importing the Blender in the code

myobj = bpy.context.active_object     #Instantiating
the object
for face in myobj.data.polygons:
verts_in_face = face.vertices[:]
print("The               Face Index", face.index)
print("Heading1", face.Heading1)
for vert in verts_in_face:
local_point = myobj.data.vertices[vert].co
worldpoint = myobj.matrix_world * local_point
print("vert", vert, " vert co", worldpoint)
```

Chapter 10 – Fun Challenge

Challenge 13

Write two codes to demonstrate how indexes for selected polygons can be obtained.

Chapter 10 – Solution

Solution 1

```
# assuming the object is currently in Edit Mode.
import bpy
import bmesh
myobj = bpy.context.edit_object
me = myobj.data
mybm = bmesh.from_edit_mesh(me)
for f in mybm.faces:
    if myf.select:
        print(myf.index)
# Show the updates in the viewport
# and recalculate n-gon tessellation.
bmesh.update_edit_mesh(me, True)
```

Solution 2

```
import bpy
import bmesh
from bmesh.types import BMFace
myobj = bpy.context.edit_object
me = obj.data
mybm = bmesh.from_edit_mesh(me)
for geom in bm.select_history:
    if isinstance(geom, BMFace):
        print(geom.index)
bmesh.update_edit_mesh(me, True)
```

Chapter 11

Python Data Analysis Libraries

Python language has gained a lot of interest in recent times as a popular choice of language for data analysis. Even though some data scientists may argue that R is still popular, the phenomenal growth and evolution of Python for data analysis cannot be ignored. If you still doubt the use of Python language for data analysis, here are some of the advantages that Python provides:

- Python is an open source. Any data analyst can download and use it.
- Growing online community of Python data scientists. The Python online community continues to grow at an exponential rate. Therefore, debugging and learning issues can easily be sorted by this large online community.
- It is simple to learn.

- It has numerous data analysis libraries that continue to grow.

At this point, you're already familiar with Python's fundamental building blocks. You can now take your skills one step further by exploring data analysis. Imagine you want to perform the following tasks.

- Multiply 2 or more matrices
- Find the roots of quadratic equations
- Plot bar charts, histograms, and pie charts
- Make statistical models
- Access web pages

Looking at the above examples, you'll realize that they all pertain to statistical analysis. Even though any programming language can be coded from scratch to perform the above statistical tasks, the process can be quite tedious and laborious. Thankfully, there are several data analysis libraries that have been ported to Python to help you with data analysis.

Python libraries

To be acquainted with Python data analysis libraries, you must first understand how mathematical libraries work in Python. Ultimately, the first step is learning how to import them into your programming environment. You can use:

```
import math as t
```

Or

```
from math import *
```

In the first code, we have defined an alias t to the Python library "math". You can then proceed to use various functions from the math library, such as factorial, by referencing it using its alias `t.factorial()`. In the second code, we have just imported the entire namespace in for Python library "math" and we can directly use `factorial()` without referring to the math library.

Below are common data analysis libraries that you'll find in Python:

1. ***NumPy (Numerical Python)***. The most powerful feature of the NumPy library is its n-dimensional array. NumPy also contains the basic linear algebra functions, Fourier transforms and advanced random number capabilities. You'll also find tools for integration with other low-level programming languages such as FORTRAN, C, and C++.
2. ***SciPy (Scientific Python)***. The SciPy library has been built on the NumPy library. It is one of the most important libraries for performing a variety of high-level science and engineering modules such as discrete Fourier transformation, Optimization and Sparse matrices and Linear Algebra.
3. ***Matplotlib***. As the name suggests, Matplotlib is used for plotting a vast variety of graphs, starting from the histograms to line plots to the heat plots. You can use the Pylab feature in the ipython notebook (using the notation ipython notebook –Pylab = inline) to help you use this plotting features inline. If you don't use the

inline option, then Pylab will automatically convert ipython environment to an environment that is similar to MatLab.

4. **Pandas.** This library is used for structured data operations and manipulations. Pandas has extensively used data munging and preparation.

5. **Scikit.** This library was added to python to help with machine learning. The library has been built on NumPy, SciPy, and Matplotlib. It contains many efficient tools for machine learning and statistical modeling such as classification, regression, and clustering.

6. **Statsmodels** This library is used for statistical modeling. The Statsmodels is a Python module that enables users to explore their data, estimate the statistical models, and perform statistical tests. It has an extensive list of descriptive statistics, statistical tests, plotting functions, and estimators.

7. **Seaborn.** This library is used for statistical data visualization. Seaborn makes attractive and informative statistical graphics using the Python language. It is built on Matplotlib and aims to make visualization a key part of exploring and understanding statistical data.

8. **Bokeh.** This library is used for creating interactive plots, dashboards and data applications on modern web-browsers. It allows users to generate attractive and concise graphics in the style of D3.js.

9. **Blaze** This library is used for extending the capability of the NumPy and the Pandas libraries to distributing and streaming data sets. This library can be used to access data from several sources such as Bcolz, MongoDB, SQLAlchemy, Apache Spark and PyTables. When used with Bokeh, Blaze can be a very powerful tool for

developing effective visualizations and dashboards on large sets of data.

10. *Scrapy* This library is used for web crawling. It is a very powerful framework for extracting specific patterns of data. It has the potential of starting at a website home URL and then digging through the web pages within the website to extract data.

11. *SymPy* This library is used for symbolic computation. It has a variety of capabilities that ranges from basic symbolic arithmetic to calculus, algebra, quantum physics and discrete mathematics.

Now that you are familiar with Python data analysis libraries, let's dive deeper into data analysis using Python. For you to become an experienced data analyst, you have to understand the following concepts with regards to data analysis and how the Python libraries can help you:

- Data Exploration. It is the first phase of data analysis. In this phase, you want to find out more about the data that you have.
- Data Munging. During this phase, you are basically cleaning the data and playing with it to make it better for statistical modeling. Determining the appropriate library for data munging will go a long way in understanding the variables that you're dealing with.
- Predictive Modeling. During this stage, you'll be running the actual algorithms to understand what your data is.

Let's now examine some of the most common operations that you can do with Python using the NumPy library.

#1: Creating n-dimensional arrays

There are several ways to create n-dimensional arrays. The code below shows how you can create a 2X3 double precision array using NumPy in Python:

```
import numpy as np
a = np.zeros((2,3), dtype=np.float64) # Generate a
2X3 double precision array that is initialized to
all zeroes

a = np.array([[0,1,2],[3,4,5]], dtype=np.float64)#
Initialize the array

a = np.genfromtxt('data1.csv', dtype=np.float64,
delimiter=',') # Create the array by reading from
the CSV file

dtype=np.float64).reshape(2,3) # Create an array
using "arange" function a = np.arange(6,4)
```

#2: SciPy Linear Algebra functions

The SciPy is one of the most important libraries for performing a variety of high-level science and engineering modules such as discrete Fourier transformation, Optimization and Sparse matrices and Linear Algebra. The code below shows how linear algebraic function can be generated using the SciPy library:

```
import numpy as nump
from scipy import linagebra
myarray = nump.array([[1, 2], [3, 4]],
dtype=nump.float64
linagebra.inv(myarray) # This computes the inverse
matrix
linagebra.eigvals(myarray) # This computes
eigenvalues
```

#3: 2D plotting using the Matplotlib

```
import numpy as nump
import    matplotlib.pyplot    as    myplot    x    =
nump.linspace(0.0, 2.0, 20)
myplot.plot(x, nump.sqrt(x), 'ro') # red circles
myplot.show()
myplot.plot(x, nump.sqrt(x), 'b-') # blue lines
myplot.show()
```

Chapter 12

Advance File Handling

In this chapter, you'll learn about Python file operations. In particular, you'll learn how to open a file, read from it, write into it, close it and the various file methods you should know in Python. By the end of the chapter, you will be able to open existing files and manipulate them. Are you ready?

So, what is a file? A file is simply a named location on disk that has stored related information. Files are used to store data on a permanent basis on a non-volatile storage device such as a hard disk. You are aware that the main memory—and specifically the RAM—cannot be used to store data on a permanent basis. Therefore, files must always be stored on a permanent storage device.

When a file is created on a secondary storage device, the following file information is automatically generated by the respective OS:

- Name of the file
- Its location
- File size
- File attributes such as read/write read only and archive

When you want to read from or write into any file on your computer, you need to first open it. When you're done with it, you should close it so that the resources that had been tied to it are freed. In Python, a file operation takes place in the following order:

- Opening the file
- Reading or writing into the file (perform operation)
- Closing the file

Opening a file

Python language has a built-in function called `open()` that is used to open a file. This function returns a file object which is called a handle since it is used to read or modify the file accordingly. For instance,

```
f = open("test.txt")
```

Opens file named "test.txt" that is stored in the current directory of the Python source code.

While

```
f = open("C:/Python33/test.txt")
```

Opens a file named "test.txt" in the folder C:/Python33

You can specify the mode of reading while opening the file. In the mode, you can specify whether you want to read "r", write "w" or append "a" data to the file. You can also specify whether you want to open the file in the text or the binary mode. The default mode is reading where you get strings of data from the file. On the other hand, the binary mode returns bytes of data. You can use this mode if you are dealing with non-text data such as images.

Below is a summary of the file modes and their descriptions:

- `'r'` opens the file for reading. It is the default mode.
- `'w'` opens the file for writing. It creates a new file if it does not exist or truncates the file if it is existing.
- `'x'` opens the file for exclusive creation. If the file has already been created, the operation fails.
- `'a'` opens the file for appending data at the end of the file without truncating it. It generates a new file if it does not exist.
- `'t'` opens the file in text mode. It is the default mode.
- `'b'` opens the file in binary mode.
- `'+'` opens the file for updating (for both reading and writing).
- `ab+` opens the file for both appending and reading in the binary format. The file pointer will be at the end of the file if the file already exists. The file will open in the

append mode. If the file is not there, it creates a new one for reading and writing.

The File Object Attributes

Once you open a file, the file object is automatically created with the following information:

- `file.closed`. it returns true if the file has been closed and false if the file has been opened.
- `file.mode`. it returns the access mode with which the file was opened.
- `file.name`. it returns the name of the file.
- `file.softspace`. it returns false if space is explicitly required with print, true otherwise.

The Python code below illustrates an example of how you can work with file object attributes:

```
myfile = open("Readme.txt", "wb")
print "The name of the file is: ", myfile.name
print "Is the file closed or not? : ",
myfile.closed
print "The opening mode of the file is: ",
myfile.mode
print "The Softspace flag of the file is: ",
myfile.softspace
```

The above code will produce the following output:

```
The name of the file is: Readme.txt
Is the file closed or not? : False
The opening mode  of the file is: wb
The Softspace flag of the file is:
```

The close () Method

The `close()` method of a file object is used to flush any unwritten information and close the file object. When the file has been closed, no more writing can take place. You should note that Python automatically closes the file when the reference object of the file is reassigned to another file. That is why it is good programming practice to use the `close()` method to close a file.

Below is the syntax for closing a file:

```
fileObject.close()
```

Below is an example code of how you can close a file in Python:

```
myfile = open("Readme.txt", "wb")
print "The name of the file is: ", Readme.name
myfile.close()
```

Reading and Writing Files

The file object gives a set of access methods that makes the process of reading and writing to files much easier. In particular, the two methods that you'll need are the `read()` and `write()` methods.

The write method

The `write()` method is used to write any string to an open file. It is crucial to note that Python strings can have binary data and not just text data. The `write()` method does not add any newline characters (`'\n'`) to the end of the string. Here's the syntax for the `write()` method:

```
fileObject.write(string)
```

Below is an example of a Python code that uses the `write()` method:

```
myfile = open("Readme.txt", "wb")
myfile.write( "I have learned several aspects of
Python Programming in this book.\n And the book is
great for Advanced Programmers! \n")
myfile.close()
```

The above method creates a Readme.txt file and writes the given content in that file. When you open the file, here will be its contents:

```
I    have    learned    several    aspects    of    Python
Programming  in  this  book.  And  the  book  is  great
for Advanced Programmers!
```

The read method

The read () method is used to read a string from a file that you have opened. It is crucial to note that Python strings can also have binary data apart from the text data. Below is its syntax:

```
fileObject.read([count])
```

In the above example, the passed parameter is the number of bytes that are supposed to be read from the opened file. The read method begins reading from the start of the file. If the count is missing, it will attempt to read as much information as possible until the end of the file.

Here is an example:

```
myfile = open("Readme.txt", "r+")
mystr = myfile.read(10);
print "Read string is: ", mystr
# Check current position
position = myfile.tell();
print "Current file position : ", position
# Reposition the pointer at the start of the
string once again
position = myfile.seek(0, 0);
mystr = myfile.read(10);
print "Again read Mystring is: ", mystr
# Close the opened file
myfile.close()
```

Looking at the above code, you'll realize that you have to create a loop in order for you to read the entire string. One easy way to read the text file and parse each line is by using the statement `readlines` with the file object. The Python's `readlines` reads every data in the text file. Here's an example:

```
myfile = open("Readme.txt", "r")
lines = myfile.readlines()
f.close()a
```

Now, the above code reads the entire file.

What about reading the file line by line?

You can use the while statement to help you read the file line by line. Below is an example:

```
myfile = open("Readme.txt")
line = myfile.readline()
while line:
    print line
    line = myfile.readline()
myfile.close()
```

Chapter 12 – Fun Challenges

Challenge 14

Write a Python program that reads an entire text file

Challenge 15

Write a Python program that counts the number of lines in a text file

Challenge 16

Write a Python program that removes newline characters from a file

Chapter 12 - Solutions

Solution for Challenge 14

```
Def file_read(myfile)
mytext=open (myfile)
print(mytext.readlines)
file_read("myfile.txt")
```

Solution for Challenge 15

```
def file_length(myfile):
        with open(myfile) as f:
                for i, l in enumerate(f):
                        pass
        return i + 1
print("Number   of   lines   in   the   file   are:
",file_length("Readme.txt"))
```

Solutions for Challenge 16

```
def remove_lines(myfile):
    flist = open(myfile).readlines()
    return [s.rstrip('\n') for s in flist]
print(remove_lines("Readme.txt"))
```

Chapter 13

Refactoring Python Code

Like it or not, bugs will always occur in code no matter how keen you are when coding your software. Despite your best efforts to write comprehensive software in Python, it's almost impossible to avoid bugs. So, where does refactoring come in?

Refactoring is a way of describing the process in which you'll re-write parts of your Python code to make them bug-free. However, don't get me wrong here, I am not implying that you'll have to re-write the entire code. Re-writing the software code means that you'll start from scratch again and create an improved version whereas refactoring is an incremental process in which you enhance the existing code—not starting from scratch—by making changes to the software in bits.

Let me elaborate on this.

Usually, regardless of what language you are using to write a software —Python included—you start by finding any working solution. At the initial stages of the development, finding that best solution is close to impossible! Since along the way, there will be many different solutions to any given problem, there is a high probability that any code that you write will turn out to either be slow or with bugs.

The process of writing the code by identifying solutions that work and improving on it is formally called Test Driven Development (TDD). TDD is perhaps the most widely applicable method of software development as it can be used in any programming language, not just Python.

In this approach, a programmer starts by developing an example of the software that can be used to ensure that the software works. Once a test case has been developed, the programmer will then focus on writing the code that passes the test of functionality with minimal or no errors. If the code passes the test case, the developer will then focus on refactoring it or on improving its code so that it runs faster, is more readable and adheres to programming's best practices.

The benefits of factoring can be summarized into the four main points as follows:

- To make the code more readable for you and other users.
- To improve its extensibility so that new functionalities can easily be derived from it.
- To reduce the runtime of the program and increase its speed.
- To reduce its memory usage.

Python Code Refactoring Tools

Now that you understand what refactoring is, how do we refactor the python code?

Good question.

If you happen to be using an Integrated Development Environment (IDE), then there is a high chance that it contains useful tools for refactoring the Python code. As there are numerous examples of Python IDEs, all I can advise is for you to carefully explore the IDE that you are using to get an idea of how it handles refactoring. You can start by looking through its documentation—especially the search features—to see how you can optimize the variables, regular expressions and so on.

If you want a more comprehensive tool for refactoring your code, then I recommend the Rope library for Python. The Rope library can be used to upgrade the features of any IDE, such as improving the process of auto-completion, adding features for automatic removal of unused or duplicate modules and accessing the Python docs from inside the IDE.

What if you're not using an IDE?

Well, if you're using VI or Emacs, then you can try out Bicycle Repairman to help you with refactoring. The Bicycle Repairman can also be used with IDEs and is similar to the Rope library as it can automate common refactoring tasks.

CONCLUSION

Programming isn't for the faint-hearted. So, if you're faint-hearted, then you won't be able to go anywhere. However, you can still become a professional programmer by discarding this faint-hearted mentality and working harder to realize your true potential. If you're reading this, I'm certain that you've already taken the first step by managing to complete this book. The fact that you've read the entire book means that you're really interested in learning Python. Otherwise, you wouldn't have been able to read the entire book.

Now, this is only the first step. Remember, you want to become a top-notch programmer. Top-notch programmers don't give up along the way! Go ahead and practice to conceptualize all the ideas that you have learned in this book. Remember, the rule of thumb in learning any programming language is practice since practice makes perfect.

I'm also glad that you've chosen to learn the Python language. There's no doubt about the power of the Python programming language. With the concepts that you have learned in this book, you should now be in a position to begin developing apps that are powerful, be it web applications, programs for data analysis or even mobile apps.

If you have any questions regarding Python language, do feel free to share your concerns with us.

RESOURCES

Web Development

Python Standard Libraries & Package Index– http://www.python.org

Module

Mechanize - http://wwwsearch.sourceforge.net/mechanize/

Framework

Django - https://www.djangoproject.com/

Pylons - http://pylonsproject.org/

Micro-Framework

Flask - http://flask.pocoo.org/

Bottle - http://bottlepy.org/docs/dev/

Software Development

Scons – http://www.scons.org/

Builddot - http://buildbot.net/

Apache Gump – http://gump.apache.org/

Roundup – http://roundup.sourceforge.net/

Advanced Content Management

Plone – https://plone.org/

Django CMS - https://www.django-cms.org/en/

Scientific and Numeric Analysis

SciPy - http://scipy.org/

Panda - http://pandas.pydata.org/

IPython - http://ipython.org/

Desktop GUIs

wxWidgets - https://www.wxpython.org/

Kivy - https://kivy.org/

Qt - https://wiki.qt.io/PySide

Plaform Specific

GTK+ - http://www.pygtk.org/

Home Automation

Home Assistant - https://github.com/home-assistant/home-assistant

OpenHAB - http://www.openhab.org/

Amazing Things To Do with Python

Everyday Life - http://avilpage.com/2014/08/amazing-things-to-do-with-python-in.html

Daily Challenge -

http://interactivepython.org/runestone/static/everyday/index.html

Free Tutorials

https://www.learnpython.org/

https://developers.google.com/edu/python/Challenges/basic

http://www.pythonchallenge.com/

Advanced Courses

Advance Python Courses from University of Michigan -

https://goo.gl/XPfw3N

Full Stack Web Development from Hong Kong University of Science and

Technology - https://goo.gl/H2mO9R

Intermediate Python Course of Data Analysis and Visualization -

https://goo.gl/2ZZczB

ABOUT THE AUTHOR

Ronald Olsen goes crazy when the latest technology and innovative gadgets are launched. His favorite sites are Kickstarter and Indiegogo. He is an entrepreneur, a part-time IT lecturer, and an author.

As a child, Ronald was curious why his dad was always hiding behind the enormous monitor. He started to ask questions on how a program works. His keen interests did not go unnoticed by his dad.

Ronald received his first C++ programming book as a Christmas gift from his dad. It is his first experience with coding and it wasn't easy for him. It was a tricky and complex journey. The content was too technical and boring for him.

Ronald did not give up and keep practicing with some guidance along the way from his dad. He created his first calculator program in 2001. It was his proud eureka moment!

Fast forward. Ronald feels that programming book should not be complex and boring. It should be easy and fun. With years of knowledge and experience, Ronald is able to simplify the technicalities with easy to understand content. He likes to add elements of fun and personal touch to his programming books for beginners to learn to code easily.

In his spare time, Ronald likes to surf and work on his app development in a café while enjoying his Frappuccino.

Ronald's Message

Thank you for reading! This book contains both the beginner and advanced guide of Learn Python Series to help you excel and familiarize with the various features, functions, libraries and uses of Python programming.

If you would like to read more great books like this one, why not subscribe to our website and follow me here.

https://www.auvapress.com/vip

Thanks for reading! Please add your honest review on Amazon

and let me know what your thoughts! - Ronald

Other Ronald's Titles You Will Find Useful

Raspberry Pi

Learn all you need to know about Raspberry Pi 3 and impress your friends with your DIY toy. Discover in and outs of Raspberry Pi without the complexities.
https://www.amazon.com/dp/B06XG1N4K3/

- You will learn how to set up Raspberry Pi 3
- You will learn how to set up and program in Raspberry Pi 3
- You will learn what is GPIO Pins.
- You will discover some of the fun, interesting and useful Raspberry projects.

Ronald Olsen
ISBN: 978-1-5441-4145-9   Paperback: 102 Pages
eBook, Audiobook Available

Ethereum

Have you come across news about Bitcoin breaking the new highs or perhaps news report about young millionaire been made with Bitcoin trading? Do you know that Ethereum is also breaking new highs too? Both are dancing in sync to the tune of the market sentiments.
https://www.amazon.com/dp/B0749RMHDY/

- You will learn what is Ethereum, the history and the vision that makes it shines brightly among the stars
- You will discover the pro and cons of Ethereum
- You will learn which is better? Ethereum or Bitcoin.

Victor Finch
ISBN: 978-1-5487-8437-9   Paperback: 126 Pages
eBook, Audiobook Available

Other AUVA PRESS Titles You Will Find Useful

Blockchain Technology

Blockchain is a revolution that you should not ignore anymore.
Imagine you are been presented with an opportunity before the flourishing of Internet, what would you do? Now is the time!
https://www.amazon.com/dp/B01N1X3C75/

BLOCKCHAIN TECHNOLOGY

THE ESSENTIAL QUICK & EASY BLUEPRINT TO UNDERSTAND BLOCKCHAIN TECHNOLOGY AND CONQUER THE NEXT THRIVING ECONOMY! GET YOUR FIRST MOVER ADVANTAGE NOW!

- You will understand everything you need to know about the mechanics of Blockchain.
- You will learn how you can benefit from Blockchain
- You will learn the **legal implications of Blockchain technology**

—— VICTOR FINCH ——

Victor Finch
ISBN: 978-1-5413-6684-8   Paperback: 102 Pages
eBook, Audiobook Available

Bitcoin

Are you still wondering or clueless about what is Bitcoin? Do you know Bitcoin is thriving robustly as a digital currency because of its characteristics for more than 8 years.
https://www.amazon.com/dp/B06XF6JK96/

BITCOIN

THE ONLY COMPLETE QUICK & EASY GUIDE TO MASTERING BITCOIN AND DIGITAL CURRENCIES

MAKE MORE MONEY WITH BITCOINS

- You will understand everything (including merits & demerits) you need to know about Bitcoin
- You will learn how to use Bitcoin and read the transactions.
- You will learn and discover the best practices in using Bitcoin securely.

—— VICTOR FINCH ——

Victor Finch
ISBN: 978-1-5441-4139-8   Paperback: 98 Pages
eBook, Audiobook Available

Other AUVA PRESS Titles You Will Find Useful

Smart Contracts

Smart Contract is about the revolutionary (Blockchain Technology) approach with legal contracts or any legal agreements. This book offers an unprecedented peek into what the future may be like that could possibly change and enhance the traditional way of doing things for the better (many benefits).
https://www.amazon.com/dp/B06XW4L38F/

SMART CONTRACTS

THE ESSENTIAL QUICK & EASY BLUEPRINT TO
UNDERSTAND SMART CONTRACTS AND
BE AHEAD OF COMPETITION
GET YOUR SMART EDGE NOW!

- You will learn how disruptive (positive) are Smart Contracts
- You will learn about the legal perspectives of Smart Contracts.
- **BONUS Highlight:** More than 7 Possible Smart Contract Use Cases in different industries.

—— VICTOR FINCH ——

Victor Finch
ISBN: 978-1-5446-9150-3   Paperback: 106 Pages
eBook, Audiobook Available

Data Analytics

Leading companies often compete on faster ROI within the shortest time but also face stiff competition in this digital frontier age. Data Analytics is a critical skills in evaluating the results and achieves your desired ROI.
https://www.amazon.com/dp/B071FM45GV/

YOUR ULTIMATE GUIDE TO LEARN
AND MASTER DATA ANALYTICS

DATA ANALYTICS

GET YOUR BUSINESS INTELLIGENCE RIGHT

FOR BEGINNERS

ACCELERATE GROWTH AND CLOSE MORE SALES

$2348

- You will be expose to the big picture of Business Intelligence Data Analytics and its competitive advantages.
- You will have a practical introduction on the four important steps in Data Analytics
- **BONUSES (Cases Studies + New Exciting Frontier)**

VICTOR FINCH

Victor Finch
ISBN: 978-1-5466-4191-9   Paperback: 128 Pages
eBook, Audiobook Available

Other AUVA PRESS Titles You Will Find Useful

Big Data for Business

Do you know that last two years accounts for 90 percent of the data in the world? Data whispers stories. If you listen carefully, process it, analyze it and act on it, to move towards your next revolution.
https://www.amazon.com/dp/B074PR6P3W

- You will learn all about Big Data and the challenges
- You will learn how to use Descriptive and Predictive Analytics
- You will learn and discover the various algorithms used in Big Data

Victor Finch
ISBN: 978-1-9739-5766-9   Paperback: 130 Pages
eBook, Audiobook Available

Machine Learning

Have you ever pause and wonder why some companies like Amazon knows what you like or browsing and make timely recommendations to you?
https://www.amazon.com/dp/B072SF1Y1K/

- You will learn all about machine learning algorithms.
- You will discover some of the applications that has been developed as a result of machine learning.
- **You will learn an important chapter that is fundamental to apply machine learning**

Matt Gates
ISBN: 978-1-5470-3904-3   Paperback: 104 Pages
eBook, Audiobook Available

AUVA PRESS

AUVA Press commits lots of effort in the content research, planning and production of quality books. Every book is created with you in mind and you will receive the best possible valuable information in clarity and accomplish your goals.

If you like what you have seen and benefited from this helpful book, we would appreciate your honest review on Amazon or on your favorite social media.

Your review is appreciated and will go a long way to motivate us in producing more quality books for your reading pleasure and needs.

Leave a review on Amazon:

https://www.auvapress.com/amazon-review/python-programming-2in1

Visit Us Online

AUVA PRESS Books
https://www.auvapress.com/books

Register for Updates
https://www.auvapress.com/vip

Contact Us

AUVA Press books may be purchased in bulk for corporate, academic, gifts or promotional use.

For information on translation, licenses, media requests, please visit our contact page.
https://www.auvapress.com/contact

- END -

www.ingramcontent.com/pod-product-compliance
Lightning Source LLC
LaVergne TN
LVHW022304060326

832902LV00020B/3265